MY GANG

By

GORDON M. LABUHN

ISBN: 1481864270
ISBN 13: 9781481864275

Library of Congress Control Number: 2013900181
CreateSpace Independent Publishing Platform
North Charleston, South Carolina

CONTENTS

WELCOME TO MY GANG

Walk with me in the dangerous world of 1940 Detroit, down rat infested alleys. Feel the thrill of power as you manipulate an enemy, feel the shame in losing dignity as you crumble under pressure, and feel the pain of death as it rips away a treasured friend.

Become a gang leader watching your back in the reflection of storefront windows, to emerge from darkness of poverty into a rich and adventurous life.

I'll be your guide, but first I want you to meet a few of my boys. Bernie, Tommy, Ted, Ron, and Mickey were early childhood playmates who never became part of the formal structured gang. Of the sixteen diehards the most active were:

Dave: From the largest and poorest family, innate, but undeveloped intelligence.

Bruce: Feisty Italian challenged everything and everyone, small of frame, but big in mouth.

Ron: Average all American with well above average intelligence, always cooperative.

MY GANG

Ralph: Master auto mechanic, driver, gutsy daredevil and protector of the underdog.

Russell: Intellectual electronic genius and adopted token wimp, shy and passive.

Herman: Gentle, strong weight lifter, judo fan, and all around nice guy.

James: Tall lanky, funny and happy center position basketball player.

George: Cooperative, sensitive, naïve, lover of booze, cigarettes and women.

Jake: Our out-of-turf area member, always supportive and ready to do anything.

If you're a tourist that enjoys travel brochures before you adventure into unknown turf, first read Puffed-Up Definitions, page 171. If you have your street feet on, come, walk with me.

Gordon M. Labuhn,
The Detroit, Michigan AFO Boys

EPISODE ONE

GLASSES

(Age 6) 1940

I organized a gang because I wore glasses. It's strange, but true.

The recipe for having a gang includes the following ingredients: One determined six-year-old child with poor eyesight and one well-intentioned set of parents who decreed that the child should wear glasses. Mix these ingredients in a 1940 bowl, throw them into the inner city of Detroit, and Walla! Motivation for creating a gang.

I was that six-year-old, and I was not happy. It's no joke having your very being destroyed by round, steel-rimmed glasses. They become a childhood prison cell. I hated them. I stomped on them, dropped them down the storm drain, flushed them down the toilet, and stashed them behind the pillar of the local bank on Detroit's Gratiot Avenue. There were a thousand ways to make glasses evaporate, and I tried to discover every one of them.

My father was a patient, stubborn bullfrog. I don't know where he got the money, but the stream of glasses was unending. He wore down my resistance, but not my will. There were times when I wished he would fall off his lily pad and croak.

I wised up, learned the lay of the land, and was able to out jump Mr. Bullfrog. He thought he had the upper hand, but I was a slick rascal. I stopped destroying the glasses and began hiding them under a rock on the way to school. I retrieved them on the way home. It was a battle of wits.

I never did learn to read, as I couldn't see all those little black marks in the books or the white scratches on the black board. So what? I could make up better stories anyhow.

I did eventually get used to wearing glasses. By the age of seven, my glasses became part of my personality. They were welded on my nose like scales on a fish, but I knew a day would come when I would be free of this hideous encumbrance. In the inner city, wearing glasses was an embarrassment, and it was dangerous. It was an open invitation to get your ass kicked at least twice a day. Besides, you couldn't catch a baseball with them bouncing on the tip of your nose. Frankly, I couldn't catch a baseball without glasses either. I decided the game was a waste of my precious time.

If I had to wear the stupid steel-rimmed pieces of glass, there were two obvious choices. I could hide in the attic and become an intellectual bore, or I could use my brain to compensate and keep my rear from being the target of every bully in town. I needed to do better than just avoid being the scapegoat's butt end. I needed to be the ramming horn, the one calling the shots, the one organizing the bullies so that they worked for me.

Walla! Organize a gang!

At the age of six, I embarked on the venture by controlling the local monsters my age. I had to manipulate them so that the games we played were my choice, at my time, in my designated location. I knew it wouldn't be easy because these boys had savvy street feet. Bernie, for instance, knew how to fold a regular old piece of paper, leaving a little hole in one end. He blew air into it, and it opened up into a little square box. He'd make two of them, numbered the sides, and we could play dice with 'em.

Tommy, who was only five, already had his own pocket knife. It was a beauty, with pictures of eagles on each side. He could take a tree branch and make it into an arrow with a point on one end and bird feathers placed in slots on the other end. We'd throw it at targets. Once it almost put out Ted's eye. Tommy carved a doll one time for his sister, but it only had one leg.

Organizing a gang turned out to be easier than I expected. All I had to do was listen carefully, decide what game the majority wanted to play, and announce my choice as a command. When anyone objected, I merely commanded the toughest kid who wanted to play the game to kick the shit out of the objectionist. It worked just fine. Within a few months, my boys stopped debating what game to play and simply asked me what the agenda was for the day. I had to adjust my communication style to insure that my commands were delivered with finesse and genuine concern for the good of the whole.

EPISODE TWO

FUN AND GAMES

(Age 7) 1941

The life of a seven-year-old in our neighborhood was similar to being one of twenty steam rollers, without a brake, on a steep hill, with a boiler stoked red hot, competing to reach the bottom first. The pitch of excitement overshadowed concern for safety and clouded our insight as to the consequences of our actions. We were not cold-hearted steam rollers, for when one of our playmates was accidentally flattened, our emotional high was crushed.

At the age of seven, there weren't any girls our age, only boys and tomboys. Only a couple of tomboys were welcome to join us in our escapades. Rita was an intimate member of our inner circle. She was a deaf mute and the youngest in a family of nine, but for us she was counted as a number ten in every way. If you wanted to have a gang of boys united into a single mind, all you had to do was be mean to Rita. We tolerated many insults and abuses to ourselves, but aggression of any kind toward Rita resulted in a united, unrestrained retaliation. We were her guardian.

In January 1941, when the streets were covered with hard-packed snow, we played hitch-a-ride. We'd hide between parked cars, and when a slow-moving car passed, we would reach out, grab the rear bumper, and slide on our feet for the full length of the block. It was great fun, as long as you didn't get your hand caught in the bumper's framework and not be able to let go.

A well-known unwritten law advised that you never grab a bumper if there was another car following. We were slightly reckless, but not unaware of the danger we were toying with.

Rita was the best slider of our pack, almost always going the full distance, from one end of the block to the other. On one slide, she hit a stretch where the snow was thin, turned turtle, pitched forward, and cracked her head against the bumper. She didn't cry. Three minutes later Rita latched onto the next car to continue her slide.

We were told the next morning that during the night some of her brain leaked out on her pillow and she died. That was my first experience with loss, and it didn't feel good. I ran home, hid in my bedroom, and cried. I think everyone did.

My parents made me put on my best hand-me-down clothes and help carry the casket. At the time, I hated my parents for making me do it. Not only did I dislike wearing nice clothes, but it was embarrassing to have the adults watching, especially when tears forced their way through my defensive shield.

At an early age, we boys were taught by our parents not to cry when inflicted with pain. The reprimands "Don't cry, you're alright, don't act like a baby," prepared us for survival in the nasty world, sometimes found within some of our homes, and almost always outside our family's protective circle. Exceptions to this being tough and impervious to physical punishment standard came as seldom as finding a ten-dollar bill. Rita's death was a sad and unpleasant experience, an emotional pain, one of these exceptions.

Ron was the only one who verbalized what I think we all felt. "I liked Rita a lot. She was real nice to me, and I'll bet she's in heaven watching us right now. If you're watching, Rita, we all love you and miss you."

There was nothing more to be said. Life moved on, even when we didn't think it could. We buried Rita in the ground and in our subconscious, as quickly as possible.

I was always looking for new adventures to cement my leadership role with the boys. The more creative the idea, the greater my influence, since unusual events were told and retold until burned into everyone's memory. Another exception to the "being tough standard" involved Bernie, a dedicated bully.

"Let's make a parachute and take turns jumping out of Mickey's tree," I said.

The tree was a big old oak with several very thick branches and not many smaller ones to interfere with a clean parachute jump.

Bernie was quick to challenge my idea. "You gotta be kidding," he said. "How we going to make a parachute?"

"It's easy. We get a bed sheet, tie ropes on the corners, tie the other ends of the ropes to a swing seat, and we have a parachute."

Bernie inadvertently betrayed his excitement about my idea. "And how am I going to jump out of the tree with it? It'll never open in time. I'll kill myself before it opens."

"Who said you're going to make the first jump?" challenged Herman.

"I did, smart ass. You want to make something of it?" said Bernie.

"I think we should draw straws," said Tommy.

"I said I'm going first, runt." Bernie was acting like he was our leader, and I let him think so for the time being, since he had adopted my idea when he committed himself to jump first. I also didn't want him pulverizing me in front of the boys.

We made the parachute and calculated that four of us would have to be in the tree with Bernie before he jumped. Each of us would hold one corner of the parachute, thus stretching it out so that it would immediately catch the air and Bernie could easily float to the ground. When we were all in the tree and Bernie was on the swing seat, we counted to three. Bernie jumped and the four corner-holders let go of the bed sheet. We were surprised when Bernie plunged to the earth like a comet, and broke his leg.

The "being tough standard" didn't apply. He cried like Niagara Falls, and we all gathered around him to provide comfort. Bernie was hurt, we were shocked, his mother hysterical, and his dad was a raging bull, stomping and shouting at us as though we had done something wrong. We thought Bernie was going to die. Our dread changed to stifled glee when we realized that bully Bernie would live for another day.

I was right about my theory. The story of the flight of bully Bernie was told and retold, but never in Bernie's presence, as the teller might end up with a broken nose. I was given the dubious credit for breaking Bernie's leg.

We learned at this early age that our friends and buddies could get hurt and die. We nevertheless pushed the boundaries by playing many games that had a degree of danger.

We liked to play Garage-Roof-Tag, jumping from one garage roof to another, but our favorite game was Duck-On-The Rock. It was another version of tag. We each salvaged a tin can from a garbage can. The person who was "it" placed his can, known as the Duck, on a flat rock. When he tagged someone, his duck had to be on the rock, or the tag didn't count. We could throw our tin cans to knock his Duck off the rock, or at him if necessary to avoid being tagged. The game was a smashing hit.

We also loved to play The Flying Chunk, a game which my dad had invented for use by the Boy Scouts. The scouts played one half of a game and my dad confiscated the game as he decided it was too dangerous. Dad retired the game to a work shop drawer. Fortunately, he never told us we couldn't play it.

The Flying Chunk was a six-inch-long, two-by-two piece of wood with the ends tapered to a point. Everyone had a 'Chunk Paddle,' which was shaped like an eighteen-inch-long rowboat oar. With chalk we drew winning lines across the pavement in the alley, about six garages apart. We chose up sides. The team to start the game placed the Chunk on the ground, at their chalk line, with one pointed end of the chunk facing the other team. The Chunk Paddle was then hammered down on the pointed end, which caused the Chunk to fly straight up. While it was in the air, a circular swinging motion of the Chunk Paddle was used to whack the Chunk at the enemy team. They, in turn, used their Chunk Paddles to hit the Chunk back. If the Chunk landed on the ground, the closest player could quickly whack a pointed end of the chunk and send it flying again. A game player was not supposed to use the Chunk Paddle to whack their enemies' butts, yet accidents occasionally happened. To win, it was necessary to whack the chunk over the other team's chalk line. This game was also a smashing hit.

Riding our bicycles down the slide in the playground at Robinson Elementary school was stimulating. We also played chicken on our bikes which proved to be a better use of our precious time because it included elements of competition, danger, and courage. Additionally, the aftermath often required a degree of mechanical know-how. Two bikers would ride as fast as possible toward each other, and the loser was the one who chickened out - turned off the collision course first. Sometimes no one chickened out, resulting in riders and bikes that needed some minor repair.

On Halloween, we strung a wire across our front lawn, four inches high, between two steel posts pounded into the ground. After dark descended, many Trick-or-Treaters cut across the lawn, tripped over the wire, and deposited their wealth of candy and coins on the grass. In the morning we salvaged these treasurers. It saved the time otherwise spent going from door to door.

Smoke bombs were also a popular diversion. We placed a photo negative on a piece of newspaper, wrapped it tightly into a cigar shape, tucked one end of the newspaper into the center of the roll, and twisted the other end into a wick. When set on fire, the bomb smoked like a volcano and smelled like burning bird poop. We tossed it onto or under a neighbor's front porch, rang their door bell, and retreated to a hiding place where we could watch the owner's consternation.

There were many other creative games and pranks we played. We had lost our snow birdie Rita, and bully Bernie had broken his leg, but up to this time we had not injured anyone outside our own comradeship. This was about to change.

EPISODE THREE

THE DUMMY

(Age 8) 1942

Developing street feet carried me from naïve assumptions to the painful realization that I could get hurt or die. Additionally, I discovered that some of my creative ideas could cause harm to outsiders of our neighbor gang.

On one occasion I suggested, "Let's make a dummy and have some fun with it."

Bruce wouldn't join in the project unless he knew what to expect and why it would be worth the effort. "What'll we do with it?"

This was one of those times that I wanted to punch Bruce in the mouth. I got tired of hearing him always challenging every idea I had. "Will you just shut up for once and help make the dummy without all your stupid questions?"

"Yeah, dummy, help us make a dummy," said Ron.

Bruce was a very colorful guy. He was a pain in the rear and often blurted out cross-haired opinions that left his opponent speechless. He veered sideways from the subject, deposited a bomb-shell insult, and acted as if the debate was over.

"You're the dummy," Bruce said. "I know you weren't born in the gutter. You had to work your way up to it."

A temporary silence reigned as our eyes bounced off the sidewalk to the sky. Ron's mammoth-cave mouth would have delighted a dentist. Extracting rotten words would be easy, even for a one-handed dentist. To avoid internal warfare, I moved ahead with my creative project.

"Ron, you find something we can use as a head. Bruce, go home and get a bunch of newspaper we can stuff into the pants and shirt. Herman, you get an old pair of shoes and a hat. What else do we need?"

Dave suggested that we needed some gloves for hands. "We have lots of old gloves. I'll go get a pair."

Bruce was the first to leave. Ron kicked the front tire of George's dad's car and walked away in a huff.

"Bernie, you want to find an old pair of pants or a shirt?" I asked.

"I'll get the shirt. We've got lots of raggedy old shirts. Mom won't care."

"George, you get the pants. I'll get some string and twine to tie the dummy together."

Our clandestine adventurer team assembled in the alley behind George's garage, each bringing the required dummy parts. It was time to reveal my plan.

"Here's what we're going to do. When it gets dark, two of us will climb into the big tree in front of George's house, sit on the big branch that extends over the street, and hold the dummy between them. When a car comes down the street, they'll wave at the driver to get his attention; then just before the car reaches the tree, they'll let the dummy fall out of the tree in front of the car."

The excitement sparked wows, laughter, jeezes, and yeah, yeah, yeahs. "It'll scare the shit out of 'em," said Bruce.

It took us nearly an hour to assemble the dummy. Our first problem came when we attached the shoes to the pants. They kept twisting around and facing backward. The problem was never solved. We decided to let the feet face whatever way they wanted. This made for one really weird-looking dummy.

The hands were fairly simple. A piece of newspaper was stuffed half way into the gloves and the other half into the shirt. The gloves were tied on with twine wrapped around the cuff of the shirt. It worked great.

The most difficult problem was using Ron's football for the head. The baseball hat fit fine, but the head's shape wasn't very realistic. A basketball would have been better. No matter what we did, the head kept falling off. When we got the head to stay for a reasonable period of time, it dropped forward—or sideway or backward—so that it didn't remotely look natural. This problem was exacerbated when Bruce, in frustration, threw the football over George's garage. We salvaged a large coffee can from a neighbor's garbage as a replacement head.

A nail was used to punch holes in the front and back of the coffee can at the bottom edge. A tree branch was inserted into the neck of the shirt. The can was stuffed with paper and jammed down on top of the stick. String was passed through the holes in the can and tied to the collar of the shirt. It wasn't a very good job, but it stayed in place enough to almost look natural.

"I've got a Halloween mask we can use as a face," volunteered George. "I'll go get it."

When George returned, we attached the mask with string passed through two additional holes punched in the sides of the can. The dummy was ready and so were we.

"It's getting late. I need to go home for dinner," said Herman.

"Me too," added George.

No one wanted to go home, but our parents would be expecting us. Besides, we needed to wait until dusk or the car drivers would recognize the dummy as a dummy.

We ate, returned, and impatiently waited for darkness to invade our world. When it was dark, we marched to the tree to begin our covert operation.

"Bruce and Ron, climb the tree and sit out on the big branch with your feet hanging down. Face the far end of the block. We'll pass the dummy up to you when you're ready."

"Will my pants get torn?" asked George. "Ma will be really mad at me if—"

Bruce slid easily into sarcasm. "Oh, for heaven sakes, grow up! Parents expect us to get our clothes torn. That's normal. I guess in your case it doesn't make much difference." Bruce's allusion to George's abnormality was either not understood or ignored by George, who held his tongue and evidently accepted the risk of a parental reprimand.

I pushed our project forward. "Ron, take this ball of twine with you. When you're out on the limb, drop down a line and we'll attach the dummy so you can haul it up."

Bruce and Ron went up, and a line of twine came down. Herman wrapped the twine around the head of the dummy, and Bruce and Ron slowly began to hoist the dummy. Just as Ron reached to grab the dummy, the head came off. The dummy crashed into the street.

"Himmelherrgottcrusemillionuntdonniviter," I bellowed. This was a word Ron read in Ripley's "Believe It Or Not" column in the newspaper. We understood that it was German, was the longest word in the world, and that it was a swear word being literally translated "God in heaven sends thunder and lightning." That was a fancy way for us to say, God Damn it! Using it made me feel intelligent.

"Jeez! Herman, help me put the damn head back on, will ya, or we'll never get this project off the ground," I said.

It had gotten very dark, and it was difficult to see what we were doing. We replaced the head, tied the twine under the arms of the dummy, and hoisted it as gently as possible. Bruce and Ron positioned the dummy between them. Everything looked just fine, except that one foot faced forward and the other backward. It would just have to do. There was no way to make the feet behave in unison.

The street was not heavily traveled in the evening. It seemed like a long wait, at least ten minutes, before a car came around the corner of the block and started down the street toward a rendezvous with our dummy. Herman, George, Dave, Bernie, and I crouched in a line behind the tree trunk.

Bernie shouted, "Start waving so they'll see you!"

Bruce and Ron waved. It was a little difficult to wave while holding onto the dummy. Bruce nearly fell out of the tree. The car passed without seeing the boys. It was too dark in the tree, and there was another large branch that partially hid them.

"Why didn't you drop the dummy?" chided Bernie. "Are you so attached that you want to keep it as your girlfriend?"

"Shut up, Bernie. They didn't even see us up here," said Bruce.

"We need a flash light or something to draw their attention," added Ron.

"I can get one," volunteered George.

"Good boy, go fetch," needled Bruce. "And don't take all night."

George was back so quickly with the flashlight that Bruce had to admit, "Hell, man! You really can do a good job when you want to." Then, just to spoil the charm, Bruce added, "It's a good thing it was a simple task."

Bernie tossed the flashlight to Ron, who didn't catch it. Crashing on the pavement broke the glass, and the flashlight wouldn't work. Bernie unscrewed and screwed the top of the flashlight on three times before he could get it working again. It took two more throws before Ron caught the flashlight.

The lights of a car came around the corner. Bernie quickly ducked behind the tree trunk, but Dave just stood there in the middle of the street, looking at the oncoming car.

"Hey, dummy, get over here quick!" shouted Bernie. As light finally entered Dave's mind, he rushed toward the tree but stumbled over the curb and fell flat on his face in the grass between the curb and the sidewalk. At least in his prone position he wasn't noticeable to the occupant of the car.

"Flash the light around," yelled Bernie.

The flashlight was aimed directly into the car's front window. The car slowed down some, but kept on coming.

"Drop the dummy, drop the dummy."

The timing was perfect, yet everything went wrong. The dummy fell out of the tree as planned, but Ron did also. The two of them crashed onto street in front of the car. The driver didn't jam on the brakes like we expected, but swerved to the right, careened over the curb, missed the tree by a foot, and came to a stop inches from George's front porch steps.

In a millisecond, tree-hugging Bruce swung down from his perch like Tarzan, hitting the ground like a bouncing ball. He limped to Ron's side and tried to help him stand, but neither of them was able to move faster than an ant. George was galvanized like an owl, looking at the car on his front lawn. The rest of us disappeared from behind the tree like gazelles being chased by lightning. Bruce stuck by his buddy Ron, even though he didn't seem to like him.

"Come on, George!" I shouted as I raced away.

George came out of his fog. "I need my pants." Sensing danger, he ran into the street, grabbed the dummy by one leg, and hot-footed his way through a neighbor's yard into the alley across the street from his home. The dummy's head and the mask fell off.

I hid in the shrubs across the street. The stunned driver fell out of his car onto the lawn as George's dad came down the steps. Together they went into the street and seized Ron and Bruce and took them into George's home. I slipped from behind the bush and escaped into the alley.

"George, over here, quick," called Herman. George made an abrupt turn toward the voice and ran straight into a garbage can. It tipped over and sounded like thunder in a closet. A dog started barking two houses down.

"Where's the dummy? Where're my pants?" He'd dropped the dummy in the excitement and couldn't find it in the dark.

"I've got the dummy," said Dave. "Don't worry. Your pants are safe."

"Bruce and Ron got caught," I said. "The driver had blood all over his face."

We sat with our backs to a garage door, each in our own world of thought. I contemplated what I had done and the consequences. I thought about the driver with blood on his face and remembered Rita banging her head then dying. I hoped the driver wouldn't die in his sleep tonight. I wondered what it would be like in prison.

George began messing with the dummy.

"Whatcha doing?"

"Taking my pants off the stupid dummy. I don't want the police finding my pants on the dummy."

We all started tearing the dummy apart to retrieve our parts. "My football's still out there," moaned Ron.

"I gotta go back," cried George. "My mask is missing,"

"Forget it. They'll think it's left over from Halloween."

Herman, Dave, and Bernie, with their dummy parts, made a trail of smoke toward home. George started back to the crime scene to get his mask, but changed his mind and shuffled toward his place. I stuffed the newspaper and twine in a garbage can and went home. There was still a lot of commotion in the street, so I went in the back door and to my room in the attic. It was going to be bad when our parents found out what we had done.

An hour later, my mom called me; I came down. She told me all about the excitement down the street. "Ron and Bruce fell out of the tree in front of George's house, right in front of a speeding car."

"What happened?" I asked.

"The driver saw them because they had a flash light. He drove over the curb instead of hitting them. The boys sprained their ankles when they fell, and George's dad and the driver took them into the house. Then police came."

"Did the police take Bruce and Ron away?"

"Oh, no. The man in the car said they didn't do anything wrong. They were just playing."

"Wasn't the driver mad?"

"Oh, no! He wasn't mad, but he did bang his head against the windshield."

"Is he going to die?"

"No, he's okay. The police say he's a hero because he didn't hit the boys."

EPISODE FOUR

THE RAT PATROL

(Age 9) 1943

Organizing the gang was easy. Molding them into a cohesive pack that corresponded to my design required creative manipulation, directly linked to our local surroundings. One of my first adventures into a more formal role of commanding officer was to organize a Rat Patrol.

Everyone knew that rats were bad things, deserving extermination. Their very existence gave us a certain amount of colorful language. A bad guy was a rat. A rat usually was assigned this demeaning title if he ratted us out, told our parents some dastardly thing we said or did. If he did it twice, he became a rat-fink, and the third time he climaxed as a rat's ass, which was much worse than a dumb ass.

Our alleys were infested with brave rats that had little fear of roaming openly in the alley, in our garages, and even browsed aimlessly across the skimpy grass in our backyards. The Rat Patrol was designed to be a community service while at the same time training my boys in the use of weaponry. We were eight years old and already behind in our fire power skills.

I slept in the attic, and one day, during my research of the dark nooks and crannies, I discovered an old .22 rifle stashed under the floor planking. To my delight, I also found two boxes of .22 caliber bullets. The Rat Patrol was not only armed but indebted to me as their benefactor.

When my parents were not home, we sat on the back porch steps and took turns shooting at the rats. Even with our expert aim, the rifle didn't shoot very straight. We put more holes in the garage than in the rats. It was considered a great achievement if we hit one before we ran out of bullets. Bruce did come close.

"Did you see that," he shouted. "I nearly shot off the son of a bitch's tail."

Herman nearly fell off the steps laughing. "Maybe you can get a tail next time. Then you can make a bracelet out of it."

Dave joined the merriment. "We can give it to Happy Bottom. She'll go leap-shit over having a rat tail bracelet." Gladys, a tall skinny pain-in-the-butt female with boobs the size of grapes, lived in the neighborhood. She was the brunt of much of our sick humor.

We wanted to do better than shoot a rat in the ass and collect tails to drape over Happy Bottom's wrist. At the corner of our block was a three-story apartment building with a big industrial trash can in the alley. The garbage was always overflowing, and there were so many rats that it would be impossible to miss hitting one. Unfortunately, we ran out of bullets and had to postpone our Rat Patrol duties until we could figure out how to get more ammunition.

"I'll put the gun away, then let's play soldiers. Everyone find some Pet Milk cans. I'll be back in a minute." I replaced the .22 rifle under the attic floorboards and hid the empty bullet boxes in the bottom of the trash basket under the kitchen sink.

When I reached the alley, George handed me one Pet Milk can. "Here's a can. You'll need to find another one yourself."

In short order we were all armed with Pet Milk cans. We laid the cans on the paved alley and stomped down hard on the middle of the cans with the middle of our shoes. This crushed the upper sides, causing the edges of the cans to turn inward and clamp onto the sole of the shoes. With cans on our shoes, we could clankingly march in soldier formation.

Once lined up in single file, I gave the command, "Forward march, right, left, right, left, left march, right, left, right, left, right oblique, march." I loved the sound of oblique.

At the oblique command, the line of marchers divided and went in several directions. "What is right oblique?" asked Dave.

"It's halfway between straight ahead and a right turn," said Bruce.

"I knew that," said Herman.

"Why'd you go left then?" asked Bruce.

"I was testing you."

"Yeah, sure."

George complained, "I can't keep my can on my shoe."

"Find a new one, dummy." Even at the ripe old age of nine, Bruce was already an obnoxious jerk.

George didn't find another Pet Milk can, but in a rusty old garbage can he did find the biggest rat any of us had ever seen.

"Let's catch him," suggested Dave.

"We can put him in a jar and drown him," said Bruce.

The excitement of catching a big live rat was contagious. The rat had gotten into the garbage can through a jagged hole at the bottom edge.

"How are we going to get it into the jar?" asked George.

"It'll be easy," said Ron, who just joined the adventure after completing a forced parental leaf-raking labor assignment. "All we need to do is ask it nicely, and it'll walk right into the jar. It's a trained rat, you know. All the big ones are. It was probably lost by the circus that was in town last week."

"Really?" said George.

"Yeah, really!" said Bruce. "Someone find a big jar and let's get this circus act on the road."

Dave found a large jar and gave it to George, who attempted to talk the rat into the jar. It wouldn't go. Dave reached into the garbage can and tried to jam it over the rat's head. That didn't work either. Dave gave it a second try and dropped the jar into the garbage can when, according to him, the rat jumped and tried to bite his hand. Herman was the only one brave enough to retrieve the jar.

We tried to strategically place the jar in the can, hoping the rat would go into it. It didn't. We tried to take all the trash out of the garbage can so it would not have any place to hide, but we were afraid to reach into the can to take out the last few gunky pieces.

"Let's put the jar at the hole where he got into the can. We can use a stick and get him to try to escape from the garbage can. He'll dash into the jar." This suggestion from Dave didn't seem likely, but we were willing to try anything.

"This is more fun than jumping out of a tree with a parachute," said Bruce.

Bernie gave Bruce a punch in the arm sufficient to bounce him on his butt. I hated to see bully Bernie get the upper hand, but it was great seeing Bruce have his big mouth appropriately rewarded.

We wrapped the jar with an old newspaper to make it dark inside, than placed the jar opening tight against the hole. With a stick we encouraged the rat to escape through the hole in the garbage can, into the jar. To our surprise, it worked. The rat went into the jar head first and either didn't know how to run backward to get out or felt safe in the dark hideout. Herman clamped the lid on before he could escape.

We punched several holes in the lid. Then we filled a coffee can with water from the hose-faucet and slowly poured it over the top of the jar. Most of the water ran down the outside of the jar, but some did enter through the holes in the jar lid. Initially, it was fascinating watching the rat squirm and try to get out.

I was having second thoughts about what we were doing. I think we all were. I didn't have the courage to speak up and stop the drowning. The first one to speak would likely be teased as a soft-hearted sissy. It was important to all of us to be viewed as tough, strong, and cold-hearted.

It took three trips to the water faucet to get sufficient water in the jar to drown the rat. After it died and sank to the bottom of the jar, we silently sat around in a trance looking at the dead rat.

After what seemed like a long time, Bruce said, "Let's put it in a bag, take it up to Gratiot, and let the streetcar run over it a few times. It'll be mush by then."

"Why do that?" asked Dave.

"After the rat's all mush, we'll go stand at a bus stop. Buses have big front windows and people sit right up front. When the bus stops to pick us up, we'll toss it against the front window, the guts will run down the window, and we'll run like hell. It'll freak out the riders," responded Bruce.

We agreed to do it because it was an exciting, on-the-edge, gangliness thing to do with a dead rat. I think it also was necessary to cover up any sensitive feelings we might be experiencing.

We executed the operation like a well trained drill team. It made an ugly mess of the bus's front window. We ran in all directions. A half-hour later, we reassembled in the alley behind my house and sat with our backs against the garage door.

"Did you see the look on the face of the old lady sitting in the front seat?" asked Bruce.

"Yeah, I thought she was going to puke in her purse," said Herman.

"The driver didn't look very happy either," added Dave.

We laughed and joked around for a while and then fell into an extended silence.

"I didn't like killing the rat," said George.

It felt like a truck had run over me, and I couldn't catch my breath. No one teased George, or said anything. We just sat there staring at the coffee can we used to transport water. A new reality invaded our world when Dave finally broke the silence.

"I think it's important to catch rats in a trap in my house, and shooting at them from the back porch was kind of fun, but..." Dave paused, "to drown them on purpose, like we did, just isn't right. When he drowned, I was picturing him as my hamster, and it made me feel sick inside."

Herman added, "It might have been a mother rat with babies to take care of."

Gloom engulfed us, and I felt like I was drowning in my own thoughts. Bruce didn't say anything, but his feelings were betrayed by watery eyes. Herman stared at the ground between his legs, Bernie wiped his nose on his sleeve, and Dave wrapped his arms around his legs, closed his eyes, and rested his chin on his knees. It was getting as dark outside as we were feeling inside.

"I gotta go home," said George.

We all headed home and the Rat Patrol was disbanded without anyone saying a word. My nine-year-old brain couldn't figure out if I had made a step forward in solidifying my leadership, but a ray of understanding light did settle in my mind, signaling the need to speak up when my feelings told me we were doing something inhumane.

EPISODE FIVE

TWO GRADUATIONS

(Age 10-13) 1944-47

Demise of the Rat Patrol didn't change the guys' willingness to have me continue determining what games we played. A gang is such a dumb thing, even when the boys are very smart. It's like the mob action of cattle driven by the whims of the wind. There's very little rhyme or reason, only a collective compulsiveness reinforced by a belief that security has been achieved. Order and structure apparently made everyone feel good and saved precious energy that could be spent more productively. We played more games for longer periods of time.

By the age of ten, I had learned to run the show without being overly visible. I became the hidden mastermind of mischief. My parents and three older brothers were unaware of the power I had acquired under the facade of childhood. Regularly attending church with my family created an illusion that screened my sham from their view.

Having my own gang, a private army so to speak, required constant supervision. This was serious business. It was an effective way of preventing my rear from being stomped and elevated my social status with the weaker, more beautiful sex. It occasionally produced free merchandise, unintentionally donated by local merchants to our cause of self-preservation and materialistic advancement.

Even though it may seem humorous that I organized a gang because I wore round, steel-rimmed glasses, I was aware that life was serious business. Humorous and serious were a mixed bag. Sometime serious things made us laugh, and humorous things put us in a somber mood. Combined, the gang's seriously twisted humor incrementally advanced us step by step deeper into a life of crime, one inchworm hump at a time.

At the ripe old age of thirteen, my steel-rimmed glasses were relegated to the back burner, hidden from sight, no longer a primary motivator. There was a bigger mountain to climb, a greater challenge. Disaster loomed on the horizon if greater structure were not added to the foundation of my gang. As our age increased, my perception of control decreased.

It was predestined that, within the year, we would pass through two graduations. First, we had to graduate from an informal, loosely knit group of boyhood playmates into an organized assemblage of intimate, dependent blood brothers. For this transition I needed to consolidate my power and bolt down recognition of my leadership. This took some time to accomplish.

Our one-to-one informal relationship was based upon unwritten laws developed and refined by usage. We needed, in my esteemed judgment, a more sophisticated framework. It was easy. I wrote a constitution and created a set of bylaws that specified how my gang members had to behave and work together as a team.

Potential resistance to the formalized structure dissolved when my father became an innocent benefactor, creating the glue that bound my boys to me. In the interest of keeping me safe and wholesome, my dad granted me the use of our family's two-car garage, along with what I claimed to be my private section of the alley. How could anyone resist being a member of an organization with a constitution, bylaws, and their very own two car garage?

In order to strengthen the ties that bind, my boys needed to obtain furnishings for our new home away from home. Stealing was not a new experience for them, but the size and quality of items desired was a stretch. It didn't seem to be much of a step into the world of crime. Within a couple of weeks, we had a lovely decorated meeting place. We acquired pictures, curtains, a fancy light fixture, a small throw rug, and even an oval mirror in which to observe our stalwart faces. We received donations of an old upright piano, a bumper pool table, and a couch that not only opened into a bed but had a hidden drawer for concealing our beer.

Winters in Detroit can be super cold. My father donated a steel flat-top wood stove so we would not only be safe from the world of evil, but safe from the cold of winter. It had four little round steel plates on top that could be lifted with a special wrench-type handle. We could even cook on it if we were desperate for blackened burgers.

Even in a garage you need communications with the outside world, but we didn't want to spend any money. Herman, George, and Russell solved this dilemma easily since they worked as mail boys for the telephone company. Herman borrowed a box of busted up phones that was destined for the metal shredder. Russell, our electronic wizard, worked miracles; he assembled one workable phone from pieces of several junkers. George dug a trench from the garage to my house and buried telephone wire in a steel pipe.

Herman completed the finishing touches by wiring the phone to a junction box in the basement of my house. It bypassed a condenser or resister, I don't know which, that controlled the phone's ringing. The phone wouldn't ring, and the telephone company wouldn't know we had it. Herman also rigged a doorbell in the garage and a button in the house. It was a makeshift arrangement, but it worked.

Calls for any of the boys went to my house, Mother answered, pushed the button that rang the bell in the garage, and we answered the phone in the garage. We always had to remember that Mother, or Dad, could listen in on our conversation if they wanted.

My Bullfrog dad didn't know how we wired it and believed that we would get into trouble. With sweet Mom's help, we convinced him that Herman's dad, who was an executive of Mr. Bell Telephone Company, told us how to wire it and that everything was peachy-keen.

The garage, which we now referred to as our hideout, wasn't very well insulated. Old Man Winter whistled through the seams of all five doors. There were large double doors that opened into the alley, double doors that opened into the backyard, and one regular entrance door for foot soldiers. It was really a stupid arrangement. It didn't take us long to acquire the materials to panel the walls and reduce the amount of cold entering our new headquarters. Our hideout went from cold to cool.

We graduated from informal to formal. We were big boys now and a well-established gang under the control of a czar. Walla! Me.

Our second graduation, becoming officially recognized in the neighborhood, was not something we thought about or even knew was important, although we clearly understood that clinging together made us feel safer when we roamed the streets. It was purely by the finger of fate that we stumbled into territorial recognition and were accepted as a mini-power-base in the local area.

Three of us—Bruce, a feisty Italian, Dave the poorest from the largest family, and I as chief in command—were confronted by a stumble bum on Gratiot Avenue. The old coot was cold, hungry, and tanked to the hilt on wine. Foolishly, he believed he could peal the pea jacket off Bruce without resistance. He was obviously no match for us, and his failure was eminent. However, Bruce and the bum both achieved temporary fame.

Detroit's finest, in a nice shiny black and white, arrived in an untimely manner. Bruce was apprehended for ripping the treasured pea jacket off the wino, and Dave and I were accused of being accomplices in manhandling a drunk. We didn't do either, but the police, or Fuzz Balls as we referred to them, seemed to think that we had. They gave the pea jacket to the drunk. We were shanghaied and unceremoniously deposited at the Fuzz Ball hangout, being destined for a night behind bars. Even a temporary confinement was not viewed as a pleasant prospect, since we didn't want our parents coming to our rescue.

The police were dumb as potatoes on a stick. They were a pushover for our pleas of remorse and promises not to do it again. We walked to freedom with a verbal boot on the butt and wounded pride.

This entrapment by the Fuzz wrapped up our second graduation, achieving for us the status of a first-rate gang. By this one uncontrolled event we gained recognition by rival collections of depraved humanity as a new power base to be contended with. This unexpected glory had a sweet taste.

We partied in our hideout, and Bruce slept overnight to wear off his stupor. He was pissed because of the loss of a pea jacket, and the rest of us were pissed because of his messing up the hideout with his stomach juices. The least he could have done was puke outside in the yellow snow. He claimed he couldn't find the door. What an idiot! I told him that he needed glasses.

EPISODE SIX

TOUCHABLE BUT UNDAUNTED

(Age 14) 1948

Not all the occurrences in the neighborhood fit into the parameter of fun and games. Some were downright ugly and detrimental to the wellbeing of man, beast, and the spirits that haunted our streets.

In addition to having mesmerized my boys into complacently accepting my leadership, I persuaded other gang leaders into accepting me as a friendly competitor. I was never invited to their strategy sessions, but was often included in their ritual ceremonies and social events. Being friendly with someone who could squeeze shit out your nose was hazard insurance for stormy days.

By the age of fourteen, I'd established myself as a gang leader and therefore believed that I was constantly surrounded by a bubble of safety glass. I didn't need a bodyguard, switchblade, brass knuckles, or magic wand. Merlin was by my side, stirring the pot that brewed invincibility. I roamed the streets with little concern for personal injury.

I often walked a few blocks up Gratiot Avenue from Mt. Zion Lutheran Church to the Guardian Angel Catholic Church, which was a large edifice with an attached school and a coal-stoked heating plant that could probably heat all the homes for a mile radius of the neighborhood. Guardian Angel also had the largest and most ornate grotto and cemetery on the east side. It was through this cemetery that I regularly traveled en route to home from youth meetings at Mt. Zion.

The cemetery had a road that snaked its way from end to end between the marble edifices. I didn't bother walking the road, but took a well-worn path between the ornate stones, several shrines with statues of the patron saints, and a few little cement buildings the size of a one car garage. I think that each building was the permanent home for as many as four important departed stiffs. The moss and vines climbing their walls made these little garages kind of creepy in the evening gloom.

On one occasion, an old man, probably in his thirties, was coming my way. I was wary as we approached each other, so I whistled a little tune and sang out a cheerful "Hi" as we passed in front of the Patron Saint Nicholas shrine. Behind the stature of good old Saint Nick was a beautiful ceramic mosaic of a guardian Angel with two children resting safely in the angel's arms. A little bronze plaque told about St. Nicholas being the Patron Saint of sick children and the guardian angel being the protector of aborted and innocent children.

I can't say for certain how it happened, but by some quirk of circumstances I ended up on my back behind the shrine of Saint Nicholas and my guardian angel. The man was sitting on my legs, holding my left arm down tight to the ground, and his right hand was around my throat.

I didn't scream like a girl or squeak like an injured pup. Instead I belted him as hard as I could with the left hand balled into a sledge hammer fist. It didn't faze him. He simply tightened his grip on my throat and grumbled, "Relax, relax."

I thought I was going to pee in my pants, but that wouldn't be manly for a ruler of a roaming street clan. I was scared. I tried to wiggle out from under him, continued to pound him with my fist, but each time I'd swing at him he'd tighten his hand around my throat and say, "Relax, relax." When I tried to relax, he lightened up on his choking grip.

He let go of my right arm so with both arms free, I taught him what a punching bag was used for by rapidly giving him the good old fashion one, two, one, two. That lasted about five seconds and his grip on my throat again became so tight that the cemetery turned red. "Relax, relax." He sounded like a damn broken record.

The man slid his hand down between my legs, unfastened my belt, thrust his hand into my pants and began a rhythmic piston pumping. It hurt. I was more than scared. I was petrified. I hated the cemetery, and where were my boys when I needed them? It hurt, but it was also a weird sensation. I involuntary rose to the occasion and for spite sprayed all over his hand and pants. It served the son of a bitch right. Then the frickin' idiot wiped his slimy hand all over my shirt. I spit on him. He laughed and said, "Relax, relax."

He stood up, rubbed both his hands on the bulge in his crotch, and calmly walked away. I was a zombie, lying there panting for breath. I didn't remember doing it, but I must have cried some because my face and top of my shirt were wet. I was confused. Why did it hurt and feel so good at the same time? Was I some kind of a pervert, a fairy? I didn't scramble to my feet or run home. I just lay there sobbing quietly.

I lay there in the soft grass behind the Guardian Angel, who failed miserably to fulfill her responsibility in protecting me. I guess Patron Saint Nicholas and the guardian angel couldn't see me in the dark on the ground behind them, or maybe I wasn't innocent enough to be of importance.

I zipped up my pants and scrambled to my feet. I looked around. No one was there, just the ghosts of the dead haunting every shadow. Damn, my shirt was a mess. I wiped it off the best I could with my hands then tried to clean my hands with a handful of grass. It was useless.

I wanted to go home so I headed in that direction, but didn't go home. I wandered the streets for a while then sat on a big metal garbage bin behind an apartment building. With my back to the wall, my arms wrapped around my knees, I turned myself into a ball. I sat on top of the stinking garbage can half the night.

About three in the morning, I went home and edged through the back porch door. A squeaky hinge announced my arrival. Quietly I climbed the steps to the attic where I slept with two of my brothers. Richard, the oldest, was awake and wanted to know where I had been all night and if I had gotten into some kind of trouble. I cried and told him what happened. He held me tight and stroked my hair. It felt good.

"Let's get you cleaned up, then you'll feel better," he said.

I didn't respond. I just did what he told me, and I did feel better, a little at least. I wanted to burn my shirt, but I didn't say anything about that because he might laugh and it wasn't funny.

It wasn't long before Richard had me tucked into my bed. He wrapped the sheets and blankets tight by tucking them under the mattress on both sides. I was a body being prepared for burial in Guardian Angel's cemetery. Frankly, I didn't care. I wanted to die.

A few minutes later, I could hear my brothers, Richard and Floyd, whispering in the other room. For a few moments it was silent, and then I heard the hinges of the back porch door squeak. I knew my avengers were going hunting. In the wee hours of the morning, they would be stalking the monument forest in search of the rabid coyote. They wouldn't find him, but that didn't matter. I dozed off into restless nightmare land.

The sun initiated a new day. As I unfastened the sticky lock on my eyelids, I gradually fell out of my nightmare world and slid back into my fantasy world of invincibility. Life in the city could be cruel. Sometimes its harshness had to be blocked out, set aside, buried in a sealed compartment of the brain, never to be opened again. Life as it was had changed for me, but its appearance was the same and must remain that way for me and my boys. There was a new dimension to the harshness of life's reality.

EPISODE SEVEN

TRADITIONS

(Age 14-16) 1948-50

My gang had well-established traditions that were fun and mostly harmless. These events and celebrations are major foundation blocks in building a lasting bond between humans. It's an even stronger bond when all the celebrants have an active part in establishing the tradition. These occasions summon strays back into the fold when other interests draw them away from their primary peer pressure group. To more fully understand how this dynamic worked with my gang, it is necessary to have insight into my charming personality, the disposition of my boys, and how we established our first annual traditional celebration.

MY GANG

I hate to disrupt a good story by inserting drab information about myself, but it's important to separate fact from fiction. I am personally a very sensitive person and do not fall into the stereotype of gang leaders, at least as viewed by today's standards or depicted on that new contraption called television. I didn't control my boys by fear or force, but by gentle manipulation. Most of the time, the boys didn't consciously recognize that they were doing what I wanted them to do. Naturally, there were times when they were out of my control and followed their own whims. I never openly fought for leadership recognition. With a couple of exceptions, the boys didn't want to be under the control of anyone, their parents first of all and a gang leader secondly.

It took a while for me to understand who and what I was. I seldom used bad language, and I hardly ever participated in stealing, although I did organize and implement the stealing adventure which became our first annual tradition. Also, I almost never got into hand-to-hand combat. I left that to others who were more physically aggressive and capable of positive results. Besides, I didn't want to break my precious glasses.

The truth is, we never considered ourselves to be a gang. We only looked like it from the perspective of other gangs and perhaps a few of the local residents. I refer to my boys as a gang for convenience and consistency of communication. Just keep in mind, we were hybrids, not purebreds.

You might wonder what this has to do with establishing a gang tradition that for years would annually summon everyone back into a tight-knit fold. Here's how it worked.

At the age of fourteen, the spirit moved me to plan an annual stealing expedition and establish a traditional celebration befitting a king. The boys were always on the lookout for interesting things that would provide entertainment at the expense of others. They didn't really want to hurt anyone, only have a little fun. This teenage need was supported by our meager economic status and the search for the scarce pleasures of life available to us.

Being a cautious, calculating leader required providing a margin of error to compensate for nature's inconsistencies. My plunge into creating the first gang tradition was no exception. The center piece of the tradition was stealing a beautifully shaped Christmas tree. I selected a Boy Scout sales lot as the provider target. It was convenient and relatively safe since a Scoutmaster would be inclined to be trusting and not suspect foul play. The Boy Scout oath would work in our favor. There would be less chance of getting caught, and if we did, we'd probably only be scolded and lectured about our sinful behavior. We'd escape the tighter shackles of the Fuzz.

Herman lifted weights at the YMCA and was the most physically fit. Jake was on the high school track team and was the fastest. Recognition of their expertise enhanced their willingness to volunteer to lift the tree. I talked with the scoutmaster while Herman, at the back of the lot, pulled a tree free and Jake ran down the alley with it. Our theft was executed without a glitch.

Multiple volunteer assignments were carried out simultaneously. Bruce, at the five-and-ten-cent store, wound up the spring in a toy car, placed it on the floor, and then walked out the front door. Dave, browsing at the back of the store, picked up the car after it sped to the end of the aisle. He left by the back door.

James and Ron each smuggled out a string of Christmas tree lights from the hardware store. They had the easiest assignment; the owner's ability to observe was limited by merchandise stacked high on the top shelf of each aisle. The most dangerous acquisition was a bottle of wine, which Tom took from a rack by the front door of the pharmacy. Russell distracted the owner by counting out a stack of pennies to pay for several candy bars and two bags of popcorn. These goodies were scheduled to be our celebration treats.

At the hideout, we celebrated the successful completion of phase one of the adventure by sharing the candy bars, popcorn, and singing Auld Lang Syne to a one-finger piano concert performed by self-taught Bruce. The boys were not happy when I prevented them from drinking the wine. I had special plans for its use later.

Phase two was scheduled for the following night, after we decorated the tree and wrapped the presents. Two strings of lights and two presents—the race car and the bottle of wine—didn't seem sufficient for a real party, especially since the boys still wanted to drink the wine themselves. It seemed wise not to push our good fortune with additional thievery. It was agreed that we would "borrow," for an extended time, one tree decoration and scavenge one artifact from each of our homes, wrap the artifact, and, by drawing straws, trade gifts.

The final phase of this tradition was an invitation to the three ministers of Mt. Zion Lutheran Church to celebrate Christmas with us in our hideout. Two of the pastors came, and we all held hands to form a circle around our treasured Christmas tree to pray. The pastors thanked God for all the wonderful things He had given us. We sang a few Christmas carols, exchanged gifts, and climaxed the celebration by presenting the wine as a gift to the ministers. They were overjoyed by our Christmas spirit.

This Christmas celebration was thus established as an annual affair, with one exception. My boys all agreed that we would not steal a Christmas tree from a Boy Scout lot in the future. Stealing from greedy adults would increase the challenge.

I never again planned or participated in implementing the stealing aspect of the tradition, but I also never did anything to prevent its execution. It was an important bonding renewal event. The boys were welded together in a lasting fellowship by what we considered a minor infraction of the law, laced with righteous humor. We didn't recognize it at the time, but it was an expression of our conflicted attitude toward power and control versus justice and goodness.

Four additional traditions gradually infiltrated our routine, growing as a result of our daily camaraderie. One became our second annual tradition, another whenever the spirit moved us, a third occurred every Thursday, and the fourth was scheduled monthly.

The second annual traditional celebration correlated to an event found in everyone's personal and family life: birthdays. We didn't celebrate individual birthdays. We celebrated the birth date we moved into our hideout. It became a great annual event. We invited our sweethearts, purchased a humongous square birthday cake and a variety of alcoholic beverages, which we sloshed down between smoking cigarettes that had been given to us free by some guy standing on the street corner. We usually held this event at Dave's house, as there were too many party-goers to comfortably fit in the hideout. Dave's place seldom had adult supervision, and his parents didn't care if we smoked or drank alcohol.

There is no end to the variety of things that can be converted into a tradition. One variable tradition occurred on average about twice a month. When more than five of the guys, and an assortment of the fairer sex, ate at the local greasy spoon, we played "Drink the Gunk." No one would admit that this was a tradition, but we did it several times a year.

An empty glass was passed around the table. Everyone put in a dab of whatever they ordered to eat. Once the glass had made the round, a little water was added. Two paper napkins were then stretched over the top of the glass and secured with a rubber band. In the center, on top of the napkins, was placed a penny. The first person to produce a lighted cigarette determined which way the glass would rotate around the table, clockwise or counter clockwise. He then burned a small hole in the napkin, passed the glass and cigarette to the next person, who in turned burned a small hole in the napkin, and thus the glass circulated around the table. Whoever burned the hole that caused the penny to fall into the glass had to "Drink the Gunk." They were not required to drink the penny.

A second, more pleasant variable tradition was watching submarine races from the back seat of the car while parked at the Detroit City Airport. Through trial and error, we discovered that the Fuzz Balls did not patrol the airport parking lot on Thursdays, thus Thursdays became our ritual submarine-watching day. It was a great way to bond with our sweethearts. It was, however, wise to maintain vigilance so that no one was surprised by unexpected Fuzz Balls shining their little flashlights in the window. The two guys who planned to become Fuzz Balls after graduating from High school were always a little reluctant to participate in this tradition, but peer pressure always won out.

Cutting deals with the Fuzz Balls was not considered kosher. We didn't allow them, with their little flashlights, to be the only aggressors. My boys and I challenged them whenever we discovered an opportunity.

Our best monthly tradition wasn't named, but I refer to it as "Fuzz Ball Buster Day." It was a very special, a close-to-our-hearts tradition that needs considerable attention.

It's important to understand that referring to the police as "Fuzz Balls" was a term of endearment, not open hostility. It was like brothers and sisters calling each other dumb names. I respected the police. I think we all did, but after all, fun is fun.

EPISODE EIGHT

FUZZ BALL BUSTER DAY

(Age 16) 1950

Being forced to wear steel-rimmed glassed at an early age forced me into manipulating my playmates in order to protect my ass, and as the years sped forward, my ingenuity in dealing with confrontation matched the pace. While intended to improve my eyesight, my glasses propelled me into a world of manipulation, creativity, and humor, especially when coping with authority.

My mental guide book for gang management required keeping my boys active and entertained while simultaneously avoiding confrontation with anyone who might dampen our free spirit. Confrontation came in two piles of cow pies: the police, who we lovingly referred to as the Fuzz Balls, and other gangs that we considered Goof Balls. I didn't need glasses to see the opportunities to be harvested by harassing these opposites, one at each end of the spectrum: the squeaky good and the smelly bad. The goal was to lead these cows to the trough, but not let them feed.

Our first venture in the harassment game came when we turned sixteen. When my boys and I acquired our drivers licenses, new vistas of mischief became the summit of our lives, being lived to the upper limit. Being petty thieves was no longer a challenge worthy of the time or energy, especially since we gave away our ill-gotten possessions. We didn't steal for money, but for the camaraderie and emotional high. We hadn't yet acquired the taste for the expensive things in life that money could buy, like a Betty Gable or Veronica Lake lookalike. Getting away with stealing something was as close to heaven as some of us ever expected to get.

Good fortune came our way through a jurisdictional policy between the municipalities of Detroit and East Detroit. The respective police departments could not arrest or give tickets to anyone not in their jurisdiction. Eight Mile Road was a major four-lane thoroughfare and the dividing line between these police jurisdictions. The eastbound lanes were in Detroit and the westbound lanes were in East Detroit.

Walla! A golden opportunity to harass the Fuzz.

We considered the Fuzz Balls part of our extended family. They periodically needed to be reminded that their authority over our lives depended on how much we allowed them to control us, plus a degree of stupid luck and timing on their part. Our positive attitude about the Fuzz Ball police was tenuous and not universal; it changed from day to day. Making fun of the Fuzz was done cautiously. We viewed the Fuzz as authorities who required our help in keeping their police skills acutely tuned so as to apprehend the real bad guys.

I decreed that the first Thursday of every month would be Fuzz Ball Buster Day. My instructions were detailed and specific. It didn't take much encouragement to convince my boys to arrange for the use of their parents' cars and to make a few minor modifications on the vehicles. At the conclusion of Fuzz Ball Buster Day, the modifications could easily be reversed.

Tail pipes on autos of the 1940 vintage were cut on an angle with the upper edge longer than the lower edge so that the exhaust was directed downward, thereby reducing the likelihood of exhaust circulating back into the car. With a pair of pliers, the upper edge was bent straight down so that the exhaust would ricochet off the pavement. A spark plug was then attached to the tail pipe with tape. An electrical wire was spliced from the spark plug to an on/off push button, which, in turn, we wired to the cigarette lighter. At each push of the button, the spark plug ignited the gas fumes coming out of the tail pipe, producing a flaming firecracker explosion.

Bumper to bumper, we roared back and forth on east and west Eight Mile Road with the exhaust echoing off the pavement, interspersed by regular spark plug gasoline explosions. We quickly got the attention of the Fuzz from both the Detroit and East Detroit jurisdictions. When the first Fuzz Balls arrived, we simply reduced our speed from eighty miles per hour to thirty, crossed over to the opposite jurisdiction, and crawled along at a snail pace. Our first Fuzz Ball Buster Day was a blast.

Unfortunately, there was one downside that I hadn't calculated into my harassment equation. Most of my boys lived in Detroit. When the Detroit police arrived first, we found ourselves in East Detroit with Detroit escorts. The police couldn't give us a ticket, but they could, in shifts, stay with us through the night. We wouldn't be able to cross the boundary line for home without being arrested.

On these overnight occasions in East Detroit, I was forced to explain to dear old Dad why I stayed out all night with his precious car. It wasn't fun, but it certainly was the lesser of two evils. Creating a logical reason for not coming home on time stimulated my creative juices. My weekly church attendance, even if just for show, had fine-tuned my conscience enough to make explanations even more difficult. Flat out lying made my voice squeak and my left eye twitch.

Yes, Dad, I know I was supposed to be home by nine. Yes, Dad, I'm sorry I forgot that you and Mom were planning to go to Aunt Edna's early in the morning. Where was I? What was I doing? Did I leave my mind in the gutter? The only question I could answer honestly was the last one. Yes, Dad, I did!

Most of my excuses didn't work. The car broke down. I called home but no one answered. Jake's mother had a baby, and I stayed in East Detroit to babysit their three sweet little children. An airplane crashed, and I stayed to help rescue the survivors. There was always the fear that my dear old bullfrog dad might check out the alibi. I knew I could harass the local Fuzz, but shouldn't mess with my home-grown Chief of Police. After all, Dad was an amateur wrestler before he settled down and became a mail carrier. My brother Floyd reminded me of this on various sensitive occasions.

On one occasion, I planned ahead and wrote a note before the Fuzz Ball Buster Day excursion. I planted the note between the flour and sugar jars on the kitchen counter. It read, "Dear Mom and Dad, I'll be in East Detroit all night. I'll call to see if you need the car, Love G." I was certain it would work if I didn't come home as expected.

It turned out to be one of those times when I didn't have to stay in East Detroit all night. Dad found the note before I came home, and when I returned with the car, he handed me my note and said, "I was a kid once too."

I figured that was a long time ago and my strategy was partially successful. He wasn't hip, and modern times had changed enough to leave a shred of confusion. Being the baby of the family had the additional advantage of three brothers wearing Mom and Dad down so that they no longer felt it was worth the trouble to debate the marginal issues.

Once I told Dad the truth, and he laughed so hard that he cried. It was the first time I'd ever seen him cry. He didn't believe me, but considered my tale of woe so creative that he discontinued the interrogation. Perhaps there is something to the saying that truth is always the best policy, although the next time he might actually believe me.

EPISODE NINE

GOOF BALLS

(Age 16) 1950

One month, the Fuzz Ball Buster Day had to be postponed to deal with a rival gang of Goof Balls. These jokers thought it was all right to infringe upon my territory and date our girls. This was unacceptable. Having a formal business disposition, I calmly arranged for a clandestine rumble to be held at Robinson Elementary School playground at seven that evening. It was a battle over turf jurisdiction. I warned the trespassers that I would include, as part of my army, all my support friends and buddies who were not officially part of my inner circle.

In our hideout, my boys wanted to strategize the details of a plan, but I announced, "I already have a plan, and we won't need additional soldiers."

My strategy was for each of us, sixteen in total, to arrange for the use of our parents' cars. Our motorized attack would be dauntingly daring with only one person per car: the driver. We would approach the school from the far end of the playground so the intruders would see and hear us coming well in advance of battle time: ground zero. Eight cars would be on each side of the playground. We would come with squealing tires, laying rubber tracks, headlights flashing, and horns blaring. We'd blow right past the school and head for the hideout without a scratch.

"This is a war plan?" questioned Jake.

"Of course, trust me. It's a creative strategy that instills fear in the enemy in advance of the battle." In truth, I didn't have the foggiest idea of how to win the battle without any of my boys getting hurt.

I knew it was essential to have a backup plan in case the rival gang blocked our exit path and we were trapped into actual fighting. I envisioned confrontation strategies on a scale of varying degrees between rudeness and graciousness. Totally rude was black, and overtly gracious was unadulterated pure white. Dark gray was as high as I was willing to go, since the plan needed to be foolproof with a level of rudeness to impress upon the Goof Balls that we were serious. Additionally, my backup plan needed to include the necessary ingredients to overcome any superior power, while at the same time being creative enough to have a tinge of humor.

Three historical facts, when sequenced from one to three, contributed to the foundation of my backup plan.

The first historical fact: over four thousand students attended our high school, which had the reputation of being a school of young mothers. No one wanted to be caught making out in the last row of the auditorium during a student body assembly sponsored by the Parent Teacher Association. Such circumstances required some fast creative explanation. To have "street feet" meant fast talking to keep parents from knowing what we were doing when out of their sight. Fast talking delayed immediate recrimination. Component one of the back-up plan: fast talking.

In the event that my master war plan went belly up, at the last moment a fast heated discussion, planned in advance, would lay the ground work for a delay in any aggressive action by the Goof Balls.

The second historical fact: an important strategic maneuver known to every war strategist is the element of surprise and getting in the first blows. This provides an advantage in any battle regardless of the size or expertise of the enemy. With a surprise attack, the battle can be won and over before the enemy knows it has started. Component two of the back-up plan: surprise.

The third historical fact: not everyone is aware that fighting has an unwritten code of honor that borders on foolishness. This code is the result of the immaturity of gangs and their failure to overcome human nature. It is certainly not a conscious desire to be ethical or gracious. This unwritten code simply stated: Don't smack your adversary if either of you are talking. This concept dictates that, out of courtesy, enemies are allowed to complete what they are saying before you beat the shit out of them. A planned violation of this rule would provide the surprise attack of my backup war plan.

It is with these three concepts in focus that I trained my boys in the "fast talk, surprise, smack" concept. I had them pair off in teams of two, talk with each other, and while one was in the middle of a sentence, the other would strike the first blow.

Bruce, as usual, became slightly overenthusiastic and dislocated a finger on Ron's tooth. Ron bled all over our pool table and turned the playing surface into a Christmas-green-and-red collage. Damn, it was hard to keep nice possessions in pristine condition with a bunch of sloppy fighters.

Thus, fully prepared with a plan and a backup strategy, we dashed off to meet the Goof Balls. It's funny how things worked out. There were at least a hundred, well let's say thirty, Goof Balls waiting for us. Our noise and hoopla evidently gave them the heebie-jeebies. They ran.

By the time we arrived at the school, only a handful remained, so we stopped to taunt them a little. The brave souls were irate when they saw my puny number of fighters. Our first Goof Ball War was won without a scratch.

I laughed at them and invited them to bring their army back for a confrontation at eight. I pledged not to disappointment them.

I said, "Mark my words. This will be an evening you will never forget."

Back in our hideout, my boys were miffed that I hadn't left well enough alone. A light flickered in my mind's eye, and I saw a way to use the Fuzz Balls to teach the Goof Balls a lesson. It delighted my inner sanctum of wisdom. When my boys heard the plan, their dour mood flipped to happy, realizing they wouldn't have to skin their genteel piano-playing hands, or mar the family car. Phase Two of my war plan utilized police power to cement my gang's status and turf boundaries.

In advance of the scheduled Goof Ball War II battle, we celebrated, since we considered our victory a foregone conclusion. We extracted nearly a full case of beer and one half bottle of Mr. Jim Beam from under the couch. At 7:40 p.m., I called the local Fuzz and told them about a big fight taking place at Robinson Elementary School. Then we wrote off the Goof Balls incursion onto our turf and enjoyed a relaxed evening of getting smashed.

The next day, rumors spread like water from a ruptured pipe, purporting an unprovoked harassment of the Goof Balls by the Fuzz Balls. It was no surprise when the chief honcho of the Goof Balls confronted me in the high school privy. He was pissed, to say the least, and tried to start Goof Ball War III.

"I don't think you want to do that," I told him. "My police buddies aren't willing to go as easy on you next time."

"What the hell you talking about?" he stammered.

Before he could challenge my alleged partnership with the Fuzz, I offered a congenial olive branch of peace.

"I'll tell you what," I said. "Your boys can date our girls with the understanding that you let me know before you ask them out." As an afterthought, I added, "And I want to be invited to your parties and have safe passage. In return, I'll invite you to our parties."

He was as confused as a tiger being challenged by a mouse. The uncertain response, "I'll think about it," was good enough for me.

"Great," I said as I turned my back to him and joined the throng of students pushing their way through the hallway to get to their next class. It was a great deal. Hell, I didn't have any control over their dating our girls anyhow, but the perception clearly established a squiggly line in the mud.

Back at the hideout that evening, I said to the boys, "I have a peace pact with the Seven Mile Guys. They can ask our girls for a date only if they clear it with me first. We're not going to sic our police buddies on them and they won't raid our place. They agreed to invite me, as a guest, to some of their parties. I have to invite them to some of our parties."

"We don't want them buggers at our parties," complained Jake.

"I don't have to invite their whole gang, just Chico, their kingpin. I doubt he'll ever come anyhow, so don't sweat it."

There was one last hill to be conquered before we called it a day: kill the fire in our stove. Ron led a charge of the light-on-brains brigade. Four stalwart soldiers semi-circled the stove, zipped down their flies, whipped out their dingle-berries, and proceeded to extinguish the fire. They pissed and it hissed. The ensuing smell permeated the pores of the walls and forced an abandonment of the hideout for a week. Stale beer and vomit would probably have smelled better.

It had been a successful war. I didn't need glasses to see and make use of the many golden opportunities in life, since I had seven years of documented proof that power and authority come to those who take it.

EPISODE TEN

OUTLAWS OUTLAWED

(Age 16) 1950

The Fuzz Ball police and Goof Ball rival gangs were not the only organized clusters of humanity that threatened our tenuous existence. We occasionally had difficulties with the intellectuals who managed the public schools and the county politicians who tried to control neighborhood behavior. The school administrators we lovingly referred to as Fruitcakes, and the politicians as the Money Bags.

Gangs, with their obvious propensity to stir the pot of controversy, heighten the Fruitcakes' and Money Bags' determination to control the spread and influence of the many Goof Ball operations existing under their noses. They decided that gangs needed to disappear, and they commandeered support of the wimpy mothers in the Parent Teachers Association.

A decree went out from Caesar Disgusted, Principal of Edwin Denby High School, that all his students must go home and be counted in the census of their biological family, divorced from and never again to be part of their gang family. Anyone violating the decree would be cast out of school and be condemned to roam the city streets in ignorance. Principal Disgusted's secretary came from on high and said, "Fear not, have great joy, from this day forward there will be peace and goodwill among all students and the PTA."

I was not concerned. This thinly veiled Fruitcake attempt to exert control over our section of the world was regression to the days of the outhouse and corncob cleaning techniques. This was a challenge to convert their decree to silk toilet paper.

The Money Bag politicians and Fruitcake school administrators were brilliant. They knew how to effectively promote gangs and violence. This was a wonderful gift, an opportunity for stupid, discontented students to exit the educational system with gusto and solidly cement their power as evil-doers in the hearts and minds of their adversaries.

Perhaps it was my glasses that gave me insight and made me so creative. My boys and I were not going to be driven into oblivion by the ploy of the Money Bags and Fruitcake crumble buns.

Even though I had a few ideas on what we should do, I summoned my boys to our hideout for a strategy session. I felt it was important that our response flow forth from a united mindset. I outlined the problem and allowed a limited, though sufficient, period of time for the boys to unload their venom before I snake-charmed them by announcing my plan for resolution of this trivial restraint.

I said, "This is what I think we should do. We should buy bright scarlet red sweaters and have a half-inch white stripe woven into the left arm." In a strategic move, I specified, "For appearance, some of you will have a separate emblem sewn above the white stripe."

As an example, I selected two potentially resistant members and said, "Bruce, you'll have a star, and Ron, you'll have a streak of lightning."

They liked that. It's amazing how a little recognition goes a long way toward preemptive pacification. Additionally, I offered to design a logo that would identify us as a "club."

"What will we call ourselves?" asked James. "A club needs to have a name."

To my surprise, Dave, not a proponent of critical thinking, suggested a name for our newly established club. "Let's call ourselves Club AFO," he said.

"What the hell is AFO?" asked Bruce.

Without skipping a beat, Dave jumped at the opportunity to expound on what was perhaps the only tidbit of literary knowledge he had somehow absorbed while sleeping through English class.

"AFO was the slogan used by the three Musketeers. They were ruthless knights. They even killed people, but were looked up to and considered honorable men. We don't kill anyone, but we sometimes steal stuff, just like Robin Hood did, and he was an honorable man too. Everyone knows there is honor among thieves, so we can steal things and still be honorable. The Three Musketeers were a mini gang—just like us."

Robin Hood and the Musketeers was a combination difficult to absorb. We had no idea about the accuracy of Dave's dissertation on the Musketeers. It didn't matter. He had captured everyone's imagination, except Bruce's, who always wanted to fight over everything.

"Honor among thieves means we don't steal from each other," said Bruce. "It doesn't mean that thieves are honorable. I still don't know what the hell AFO means."

"It's a slogan. It means 'All For One and One For All.' You read it forward and backward." Dave was fully in control of this debate.

It wasn't often that we were stunned into silence, but it was so quiet you could have heard a beer bottle drop. We just ignored the thievery aspect of our existence because we liked the idea of being honorable. It didn't take us long to recognize how great we were. We agreed to name ourselves Club AFO and, in so doing, also accepted the responsibility of buying bright scarlet sweaters.

"So, how is having a sweater going to help us from being kicked out of school?" Obviously, Bruce wasn't persuaded easily.

"It's simple," I told them. "We wear them to school, right under the Fruitcakes' intellectual noses, and they think we are some kind of an official community club."

I had learned never to allow discussion on an issue that might prove to be embarrassing, so I immediately changed the subject. "Now, you all know that you cannot give your sweater to your girlfriend."

This pronouncement stirred up considerable controversy, but reluctant agreement was reached after Herman, who didn't have a girlfriend, supported my pronouncement with a threat to beat to a pulp anyone who violated this condition. It always pays to have a bully back up a ridiculous rule.

We ordered our sweaters through a catalogue; I designed a logo and arranged for it to be made. The sweaters, with the logo attached below a pocket, arrived three weeks later.

The boys were apprehensive about wearing their sweaters to school. It was one thing to have a plan, and another to implement it, especially if it might result in expulsion. The truth is, with the exception of Russell, none of us were getting very good grades, nor did we want to be in school in the first place. No one would admit it, but we stayed in school because we didn't want to disappoint our parents.

"What are we going to do if someone challenges our club's official existence?" asked Russell. He was the only one of us smart enough to get good grades in school. He was our club geek, our weak link, our designated wimp. We only took him into the gang because his sister was being terrorized by other gangs, and she was Jake's girlfriend. We were a protective shield for Russell and his sister. He didn't need a sweater to stay in school, but he did need the gang to keep him safe.

Once again, it seemed wise to avoid answering Russell's question, so I make another profound announcement to distract Russell and provide minimal credence to our claim of respectability. "I'll arrange for Hopkins Studio to take a group picture of us wearing our sweaters. We need to figure out a date and time that works for everyone."

My boys struggled through a drawn-out debate before reaching agreement to have a picture taken and setting a day and time. The biggest problem was dealing with three of the boys who didn't buy sweaters. The cost simply wasn't in the cards for them. It was agreed that they needed to be in the picture, sweater or not. After all, it was All For One and One For All.

Bruce wouldn't let go of an idea, because he enjoyed arguing as much as physical fisticuffs, and Russell wouldn't let go because he was too smart to be fooled easily. Russell asked again, "I still want to know, what are we going to do if someone challenges our club's official existence?"

I couldn't avoid or ignore Russell twice. I said, "Don't worry about it. I'll take care of it when the time comes. You'll never be asked when I get done talking to the Fruitcakes."

Russell wasn't satisfied, but when faced with confrontation, he wimped out, asked no more, and sulked in the corner.

Life is not always simple. Sometimes it's necessary to consider the circumstances and mores of the time. Thus, it's important to understand the school's sheep farming system. While some sheep were led by the nose on a daily basis, there were those who hated school, or were too dumb or lazy to be effectively corralled in the classroom pens.

The Fruitcake farmers devised a special co-op program of lower learning in which these black sheep worked two weeks at a local business and then twiddled their hoofs in the pen at school for two weeks. Based on a good employment record and their level of cooperation while penned up, the sheep were rewarded by the Fruitcake farmers' forging on the report card grades as high as "B" for classes such as Physical Education and "C" for classes like English and Math. Four of us worked for Mr. Bell Telephone Company in the heart of down town Detroit.

There was an uneasy waiting period before anyone wore their sweater to school. No one wanted to be the shining light that might be snuffed out by a stoolie or accidental collision with a Fruitcake. As shepherd of my jolly sheep, it was by design that I, without pretense or announcement, be the first to leap over the half-asleep Fruitcake farmers.

I wore my bright scarlet sweater to school and set up an appointment with the school counselor to discuss my future goals after achieving my degree in lower education. The counselor informed me that my poor grades and the fact that I was not enrolled in the college prep program made it almost impossible to obtain entrance into any college. After the standard rhetoric and encouragement to upgrade my efforts, he asked, "What is Club AFO?"

"Oh, it's just a bunch of guys that go to Mt. Zion Lutheran Church," I said.

"That's wonderful," he said. "I'm glad to know you are staying clear of the terrible gangs that are causing so much trouble in our neighborhood."

All my boys wore their sweaters to school the next day.

There was one flaw in my strategy. Before the end of the week, only four of us still wore our sweaters to school. The others were draped on the shoulders of the lambs of the flock. None of my boys seemed to remember my order that the sweaters could not be loaned to their sweethearts. Looking through glasses of my heart, I made the wise decision not to press the issue. Losing in a little way was a small price to pay for maintaining the appearance of control.

Now that we wore a cloak of honor, we had to act honorably. This meant that we should not steal anything that we didn't need or destroy anything that we stole. When we no longer needed what we stole, we should give it to someone else who needed it. Sharing our wealth with the less fortunate would make us feel good. I don't think anyone was very hip about stealing, and what little we had done as a group in the past was considered bygone history. We were moving in a new direction.

Now, gangs are not pure in anything, and my boys hadn't been pure thieves either. Our horizon expanded to include a multitude of challenging experiences. We weren't just any old run-of-the-mill riffraff. We were an important club, an assembly of like-minded young men, casually growing to manhood by experimentation in the various pleasures of life found in our neighborhood. We were outgrowing the pleasure of stealing, since it was too easy, and we really didn't know what to do with some of the junk we accumulated in our clubhouse. Most of the boys bragged more about stealing than was justified, since only a couple of the guys were considered pro stealers.

Changing our status to being a club not only changed our attitude toward thievery, but brought into focus a changed vision of our role as males. The female gender loomed on our horizon as a more worthy target for our attention.

To maintain a modern-day tradition of the three Musketeers, the boys talked about doing things in sets of three. This included triple dating rather than double dating. I expected the guys who still had their sweaters would lose control of them any moment.

High schools have two names: one carved in cement and usually found above the front door, and the other an indication of its community-wide fame engraved on the general population's conglomerate mind. Edwin Denby High School was the technical name, but as previously mentioned, it was more broadly known as the school of young mothers. We didn't have to consciously select our new direction. We had lots of advice, encouragement, and natural incentive to engage in sexual pursuits. It was our new challenge of the day.

Personally, I avoided intimate sexual relationships even though they were prevalent in our community. I wasn't afraid, though my earlier sexual encounter in the cemetery may have dampened my eagerness to venture into the sexual deep-sea. My religious training also slowed me down. I quickly discovered advantages to preserving the ultimate pleasure for the right time and place. I understood that if you chase a dog, it will run away from you, and if you run away from a dog it will chase you. When you want to be caught, you simply have to run away and adjust your running speed so you get caught at the appropriate time. My resistance to having an intimate sexual relationship was like advertising a product that, when procured, would transform the owner: a wallflower into a bouquet, a reject into a treasure, a commoner into a queen. This increase in my popularity with the fairer sex also elevated my prestige with my boys.

EPISODE ELEVEN

TRIAL OF TEN

(Age 16) 1950

Have you ever noticed how people divide their organizations into a ladder with an upside-down philosophy, it being good to be up and bad to be down. Hell, you can't fall very far when you're on the ground, and if you do, it doesn't hurt very much. Now, the guy at the top has some real problems. It's a long way down, and he's very easy to identify as the leader or boss.

The ladder used by tycoons has the Chief Executive Officer or CEO at the top and the deputy director next in line. In the business world and politics, they like President, Vice President, and so forth. I kind of like the "vice" title. On the bottom rung of the business ladder are the workers. At the bottom of gangs, we have the soldiers, with the one called "asshole" being the absolute bottom.

I decided to invent some new titles consistent with my boys' personalities. My first thought was to consider renaming our ladder using a deck of playing cards. Obviously, I'd have to exclude the Queen since none of the boys would want to be called a Queen. I would be the King, followed down the ladder by Jack, Ten, and so on until I came to the bottom, which would be the dumb Ace. It would be nice to be a King, but using card names did present a couple of problems. There were sixteen of us, and only twelve cards in the deck after you removed the Queen. Not having enough cards in the deck was an appropriate problem since we occasionally played as if we didn't have a full deck anyhow. I could reach the needed sixteen by naming four of the boys club, heart, diamond, and spade, but that would give a whole different meaning to the ladder of success.

For a brief time, I figured I could create a stratification using the names of fruits with an apple at the top and a prune at the bottom, but I quickly realized that I didn't know how to divide up the rest of the fruits. Besides, fruits are such dumb things. Who would want to be called the banana or peach? It only took a short time to realize that fruits are little more than cutups sitting around waiting to be devoured by a stranger.

I wondered if I could use a collage of foods in combination with animals. After all, our society is designed with a "top cheese," which would be me. There is the "bottom feeder," that would be Russell, our wimp, and there are the mass of mice in between. I vaguely understood that a society with three levels—a small, powerful, wealthy contingent at the top; a large, unidentifiable group in the middle; and a small, poor, and weak group at the bottom—was healthy, peaceful, and seldom provoked an uprising. Unfortunately, sometimes a rat gets mixed in with the mice in the middle and they all want to eat the cheese.

It's interesting how my gang, without anyone having a title, mirrored the world. We had an unwritten, unspoken, but well-known ladder, and as far as I was concerned, we also had a refined method of knocking the guy off at the top for a crash to the very bottom. I'm not certain the boys even knew it existed, though they implemented it effectively.

For lack of a written description, I referred to it as the Trial of Ten. It wasn't really a trial, and ten wasn't a definitive number since no one counted. There wasn't a judge, attorney, jury, or any formal rules. It was more like a judgment by brute force, the pounding in of a tack with a sledge hammer. The first time we held the trial, a few fuzzy rules were assumed for use in future trial events. It was how the leader of my gang could be toppled from the throne.

Bruce was the first of my gang to initiate the Trial of Ten. Right in the middle of eating a pepperoni pizza in the hideout, he blurted out, "Labuhn, let's fight."

I was astounded, and the boys were watching me to see what I was going to do. I didn't really want to fight, but I felt I was approaching a crossroad of some kind. I said, "Okay, if you want to have your brains bashed in, I'm willing to do it for you."

Bruce wasn't the shy type. I don't think he really wanted to physically fight even though he wanted to verbally fight about anything and everything all the time. He was short and scrawny and not physically a powerhouse. The only big thing about him was his mouth. I think physical fighting made him feel big, even if he didn't win the fight.

I looked forward to the event. Bruce was an ideal candidate on whom I could develop some fighting skills, since fighting didn't come naturally to me. Bruce was a five-foot-five, one hundred-thirty-pound lightweight who moved at high-velocity when motivated. He was a speeding train with an empty coal car; he'd burn out quickly.

For spice, I added a prize for the winner. I said, "Okay, Bruce, I'll fight you, but whoever wins gets to choose a punishment for the loser." The disposition and creativity of the winner were the only restraints when determining the loser's punishment.

Pipsqueak Bruce did his best. He flailed in all directions, swinging his arms like a windmill and moving his legs as though he had ants in his pants, which was more than I gave him credit for. I didn't hurt him much. I dumped him head first into a garbage can, rubbed his face in a manure pie left by the black alley picker's horse, and stuffed a rotting tomato in his ear: innocent stuff like that. While we fought, the rest of the boys tossed pennies, threw switchblades and other toe stabbers at the garage wall, or just flopped around the garbage cans in the alley. Bruce uncled at least ten times and added the caveat, "I've had enough."

I had survived ten fights and deemed each a trial of my leadership. Nothing more was said, and I assumed that I had retained my position as top dog on the ladder, but a system of leadership transition was being developed. I came to the conclusion that the unwritten rules were different for me as leader than for Bruce, the challenger.

For challenger Bruce, a round lasted three to five minutes, as judged by how long it took before he cried "uncle." The lackadaisical gang members could have timed the rounds like they do in a prize fight, but they didn't exhibit any interest in establishing any formal etiquette. The fighting continued until the challenger cried "uncle" ten times, or admitted that he had enough, in which case the leader retained the throne.

I figured that if I, as leader, had given up and cried "uncle" any time before completing round ten, the fight would be over immediately and the challenger would be judged to be the winner and new leader. There was one additional possibility. I might have lost all ten rounds but not cried uncle. In that case, I believed that I would have retained leadership regardless of my lack of fighting skills or battered physical condition.

George reminded me about the punishment pronouncement to be issued by the winner. "I think you should give him a nasty punishment for being such a prick," said George.

Everyone agreed that a befitting punishment imposed by the winner would be an enjoyable encore. They waited with bated breath to see what punishment Bruce was to experience. It had been a fun experience for me, and I wasn't vindictive, so Bruce's punishment was issued more from amusement than from anger.

I said, "From now on, every time Bruce interrupts anyone at a meeting, he will be fined twenty-five cents rather than ten cents as required in our by-laws."

The boys were disappointed, but for Bruce this was a disaster. Not only did he always want to fight, but he always wanted to talk when someone else was already talking. His big mouth would keep our coffers filled with enough cash to buy our monthly supply of beer. The problem was, he only paid when forced to by thirsty boys with empty pockets.

Not every fight I had with one of my boys had as wholesome an outcome. My second trial didn't take place for over a year. It was instigated by Herman, who was a student teacher of judo at the YMCA, and he lifted weights for fun. Herman was my size, just a smidgen under six feet tall, but he had broad shoulders and rippling muscles. He was a mirror image of Dick Tracy, square jaw and all.

Herman was hard for me to figure out. I viewed him as a strong, sweet teddy bear that all the girls loved. It was nearly impossible to make him mad, and he never fought with anyone. He didn't have to. We all knew what damage he could do if he was angry.

On one occasion, some goof balls from the Seven Mile Road Gang gave us a hard time over some silly issue I can't even remember. I recall that as they sped away Herman grabbed their car door handle, ripped if off, and, in a synchronized flowing move, tossed it so accurately that it bounce off their car's rear window. It was very impressive.

Obviously, being challenged by Herman did not bode well. I won't waste your time with the embarrassing details. Suffice it to say, I lost every encounter with Herman and my boys enjoyed the show immensely.

I think the counting of trials from one to ten was sloppy. I was a mop Herman used to sweep the alley. If my ego had been made of glass, it would have been shattered to pieces, but it was made of stainless steel. I survived ten plus beatings with considerable damage to my ego, my clothing, and my body. I had so many cuts and scrapes that I looked like a freshly boiled lobster, and felt like it too. Not once did I say "uncle;" thus I lost every fight, but won the battle. Out of respect, I retained control of the bunch of idiots that laughed at my temporary, unfortunate circumstance.

I lay on my back in the middle of the alley, wondering why the sky was so red. I didn't have any advance agreement with Herman that the winner would choose a befitting punishment for the loser, but Bruce remembered my deal with him and his punishment. Bruce succinctly asked, "What do you want us to do with this bag of crap that just beat the shit out of you?"

Bruce wasn't always politically correct in his pronouncements and questions, but he certainly knew how to get to the point and sever the carotid artery.

At the moment, my wish was to send the whole bunch to the butcher, have them chopped into tiny pieces, and fed to any stray dog that was so hard up that it would gobble them down without throwing up. I considered telling them to kill the son-of-a-bitch, but I was afraid they might do it.

I was tempted to be vindictive. I closed my eyes and thought, *It's wonderful having buddies with such a high level of sympathy and loyalty. Yeah, right!* My body wasn't functioning very well, but my mind was still in touch with reality. I remembered my walk through the Guardian Angel Catholic Church cemetery and the feeling of being vulnerable and unable to protect myself. I didn't want that to happen again, so my pronouncement was, "Leave him alone. From now on, Herman is going to be my bodyguard."

"Shit," Bruce said, "you ain't got much of a body to guard."

For a moment I reconsidered, thinking I might be better served by having Herman sweep the alley with Bruce's shaggy mop of hair. *Oh, hell, leave well enough alone,* I thought, so I did, but Herman didn't.

"Shut your trap, loser," said Herman.

"Shut your own, stupid. You're just a muscle-bound jerk with sawdust in your head."

Instead of mopping the alley with Bruce, Herman calmly responded, "Stick it where the sun don't shine. That way your brain will have company."

"Enough," I groaned. "Someone help me up." I felt like I was floating on cloud eight, the black ball on my pool table temporarily in my pocket, out of the game.

Herman virtually picked me up like a broken toothpick, carried me like a china doll into George's backyard, and propped me against a big oak tree. I lay there like a fallen apple wondering if being a gang leader was worth feeling like apple sauce. I thought, *Herman has always been a loyal member of my boys, and now he's a grateful, dedicated kingpin, holding the boys together in a unit that no longer has any interest in challenging my leadership. I'm protected from insiders as well as outsiders.*

I reflected on my ladder of success theory. It needed more thought. I wondered, *If I consider Herman a kingpin, does that make me the big wheel and my boys the spokes? Does everything fall apart if the king-pin pulls out and leaves the gang? That doesn't work. Herman's not the kingpin, I am. He's not even second in command. He's more like the top of the bottom. Forget it. Leave it with my being a figurehead leader at the top and everyone else bouncing around in the middle, taking turns making decisions. With a large middle class, the top is not very high, and I don't have so damn far to fall that way. I didn't even know if I was on top, or only thought I was.*

EPISODE TWELVE

THE BREAK-IN BROKE IT

(Age 16) 1950

Gangs sometimes do things that are not acceptable to society. Local authorities tend to retaliate with punishment rather than graciously understanding the need of youth to expend their pent up energy in creative ways. My boys were normal according to the code of innocent trouble-makers.

A case in point occurred when I was desperately seeking an outlet for my bored and restless clan. We embarked on what turned out to be a successful failure. We succeeded in our plan, but failed in having a clean escape.

At two o'clock in the morning, three days before the Christmas school break and the day before the school's annual Christmas concert, we jimmied open a side door of Denby High School.

"Okay, guys, we're here to make history, not break or destroy anything," I said.

"Spoil sport," needled George.

George, Russell, and I, as members of the Denby High School stage crew, were familiar with the fly system of ropes, pulleys, and steel weights stacked in cradles. It was called a "fly system" because, by pulling a rope, you could make a curtain, a wall of a stage set, or a bar mounted with spotlights fly up toward the ceiling, out of sight of the audience. If a curtain weighed a thousand pounds, there would be a thousand pounds of steel weights in the rope and pulley rack to counterbalance the curtain; thus the curtain would travel up and down with little to no effort.

The steel structure of Denby's fly system was three stories high with a three-foot-wide catwalk at the top. As I recall, every four feet, from the floor to the top, there was a horizontal steel crossbeam. To impress our non-stage crew buddies, George and I demonstrated how to climb the steel frame and, halfway up, holding onto a rope, swing out over empty space as far as the rope would allow. We landed on the nearest horizontal crossbeam on returning to the steel frame. It was great fun.

On this break-in occasion, our goal was to make history by changing the pulley system in such a way that the grand curtain would fly up rather than open from the center to the side as was its normal path of travel.

Bruce asked, "Which rope is for the grand curtain?"

"It's the rope way at the far end, back by the wall," I said.

"Why is the front curtain rope way in the back?" he asked.

"'Cause we never use it. The front curtain rope is in the back and the side curtain ropes alternate with the center curtains' ropes."

"I've got it," said Bruce. "We're going to pull up the front curtain from the back rope. We'll leave down the sides and the center ropes, which are in front of the back rope, which pulls up the front."

"Very good," I said, knowing that it pays to compliment the boys once in a while. "We'll climb up a side curtain rope in the center, in front of the center rope so we can rearrange the back rope, and pull up the front curtain from the back."

"Yeah! Sure! I don't know what the hell you're talking about. Just tell me what to do, and I'll do it."

It took some time to accomplish this, as several of the boys were not familiar with the fly system or were afraid to hang suspended by ropes two stories above the stage. Working in the glow of red exit lights didn't help alleviate their anxiety.

Bruce complained, "I don't know what the hell I'm doing, and I can't see to do it. Whose dumb ass idea was this anyhow?"

"Shut your yap, shit head," instructed Herman.

"Thanks," I whispered. I appreciated not having to openly claim credit for this dumb ass idea.

Our plan went off without a hitch. No one fell off the fly system, there was no blood on the floor, and the grand curtain flew skyward at the easy pull of the rearranged rope system. By taking pictures of the grand curtain at several levels of height from the floor, without any of the boys visible, we documented this historical event and protected our anonymity. Mission accomplished.

It was five in the morning before we were able to return the grand curtain to its horizontal travel. At five-thirty a.m., we slipped out the side door and returned to the hideout to celebrate. We had been successful on all counts: entering, doing, and leaving without detection, mishap, or damage to any school property. Later that day, in the darkroom built by my brother in the basement of my home, I developed and printed the pictures we had taken after flying the grand curtain.

Little did I know that the night's adventure would come back to haunt me personally. Being the fall guy was one risk of leadership I had not counted on. I had made the false assumption that the fall guy was always one of the rank and file, never the leader of the pack.

The Denby High School annual Christmas concert was the largest event sponsored for the sole benefit of the parents and friends of the students and community. Denby's auditorium seated close to five thousand. So many people attended the Christmas concert that it was scheduled twice: at two o'clock in the afternoon and again at six in the evening.

The stage was set with enough chairs to fill the gym. The band and three choirs needed to be accommodated, as well as two grand pianos. It was an inspiring and festive occasion.

I served on the stage crew as the electrician. I set up the lighting system for the concert: dimmers, lighting arrangements, and spotlights with color gelatins of all shades and colors.

The auditorium was nearly full. A few stragglers were inching their way into the crowded rows of seats. The band was seated in the center of the stage behind the closed grand curtain. Around the band was a half-moon-shaped, five-tiered, three-foot-wide platform with chairs. The choir, a men's quartet, and the women's glee club filed in from both sides and stationed themselves on the platform in their assigned positions. The band conductor and choir director stood on the conductor's four-foot square riser at stage, front center, reviewing final details of the pending performance.

The stage crew was ready at the fly system to pull the proper ropes at the designated times to raise and lower different backdrop scenery to coordinate with the theme of various musical renditions. Others were prepared to roll the grand pianos to stage front center for a specialty piano duet. Stage crew members were in the booth preparing to hone in with pink-gelled pinpoint spotlights on soloists. From the booth, a stage crew member monitored and adjusted several microphones, some of which were stationary, some portable, and some were suspended from a light bar controlled by the fly system.

The bewitching hour had come. The choir director slipped off stage, front left. The conductor stood on his raised platform, and with his arms signaled for the band to come to a state of silent statue-ism. I dimmed the house lights to a faint glow, and when the audience became quiet, the Denby High School principal walked in front of the closed grand curtain to center stage.

At the strategically placed microphone, the principal began to welcome the concert guests. His first words resulted in an ear-busting squeal from the overly high volume mike. The stage crew sound technician reduced the volume control. The principal began again with an apology for the squeal, but no one heard him because the volume was turned so low. Gradually, the volume was increased to a nearly reasonable level.

To vigorous clapping and a few inappropriate cheers at the conclusion of the welcome address, the principal exited stage right and down five steps to take his place in the front row of the auditorium.

A curious stage crew member grabbed a handful of the grand curtain to pull it back far enough to take a peek at the audience. Curiosity may have killed a cat, but this night it only killed the annual Christmas concert.

To the delight of some and consternation of many, five tons of grand curtain slowly descended to the stage floor, stopping only after creating a five-foot-high pile of beautiful dark maroon fabric across the front of the stage. It was Denby High School's version of the Berlin wall, separating the kids in the band and choir from their families in the audience.

The Principal returned to the stage, but he couldn't communicate to the audience, as his strategically positioned microphone was crushed under the Grand curtain. Climbing over Mount Grand was evidently not his idea of dignity. He just stood there with his back to the audience in stunned admiration of the spectacle before his glazed eyes.

The conductor came to the rescue. With a handheld mike, he apologized to the audience for the failure of the equipment, cancelled the concerts for the day, which actually turned out to be for the Christmas season, and sent everyone home. It was the shortest and quietest Christmas concert in history. It was perfect. Not one false note was played, nor did anyone sing off key.

I brought up the house lights so our guests would not stumble or fall as they departed the crime scene. One smart ass shouted, "Encore, encore."

Our clandestine mission to fly the grand curtain had crashed down at our feet, transforming our success from historical to hysterical. I treasured a successful and humorous prank, but I didn't grasp the magnitude of repercussions associated with the finale. The end of this memorable night was the beginning of a nightmare for me.

The day after the grand curtain crashed, there was a great deal of joviality among the students, but no sign of concern or activity by the Fruitcake administrators or school staff.

The day before Christmas break, I arrived at school moments after the final morning bell rang, signaling the start of the first classes of the day. I dashed to my locker in the cage, back stage. Before I could hang up my coat, the public address system boomed an important announcement into every nook and cranny of the school, including the showers and gym.

"Mr. Gordon Labuhn, report immediately to the principal's office. Mr. Gordon Labuhn, report immediately to the principal's office."

There are many ways to become popular, but having your name prefaced with "Mr." in a command broadcast to over four thousand students the first thing in the morning doesn't bode well. It's an announcement to the world that you're in deep trouble and may soon join many former students as a branded misfit.

No matter what prompted this incursion into my world, I knew that a bold but innocent demeanor would be my best defense. I marched into the administration office and announced to the secretary, "I understand the principal needs my assistance."

"Not exactly," she said. "Have a seat, please, and don't crap in your pants."

I've never heard such bad language in the school office before. It sounds like she's pretty angry. It's amazing how some adults have no sense of humor and are so crude, I thought. Without the normal sweat-producing waiting period, I was, within a few minutes, ushered into the principal's inner sanctum.

"Have a seat, Mr. Labuhn."

Mr, again. I don't like your tone or lack of foreplay. What are you so pissed about?

Across the front of his desk, he spread, one by one, seven pictures of the grand curtain several feet off the stage floor. "Tell me, what are these?"

Acting innocent isn't going to work. Maybe stupid will do the trick. "I don't know."

"Mr. Labuhn, what does it look like?"

He isn't going to give up easily. He's smarter than the average Fruitcake. I need to stall and figure out his game. I said, "Well, let's see now." I picked up one of the pictures and studied it carefully. I turned it upside down, looked at from a side view, and finally said, "It looks to me like the grand curtain in our auditorium. What's it doing up off the floor?"

"You tell me."

"Is this some kind of a test or something? How would I know?"

With a shit-eating grin, he said, "You tell me. We found these pictures in your locker behind the stage."

Damn, caught by my own historical documentation. "Well, sir. It is the grand curtain on our stage. These pictures are documentation of an event I call the Grand Arising. It will go down in history as Denby's most unique event of 1950."

"Really? And tell me, who was the genius who created this glorious event, which caused safety chains to fall off, heap five tons of curtain on the stage, cancel the Christmas concert, and cost the school five hundred dollars to fix."

The gig's up. It's time to pay the piper. "I did it, sir."

"Really," he said, "and who helped you?"

"No one, sir, I did it all by myself." *Maybe being polite will help,* I thought.

"Yeah right! Tell me another fairy tale. Who helped you?"

A very long browbeating kangaroo trial ended with my insistence that I flew the grand by myself. I was judged guilty, expelled from school, sentenced to a life of freedom, and sent home with a parting wish from the principal. "Mr. Labuhn, have a nice Christmas and a happy New Year."

My parents and Denby's paid stage technician believed I had nothing to do with the caper. They pled my case. I was pronounced innocent by reason of fear. They believed that if I squealed, I would be beat to a pulp by whoever really committed the crime. The principal reneged, and I was pronounced innocent and sentenced to confinement in the school classroom prison. My freedom lasted one day longer than the Christmas break. I did, in fact, have a very merry Christmas.

EPISODE THIRTEEN

INTERNAL AFFAIRS

(Age 16) 1950

A great deal of gang life spins around external forces, with the Fuzz Balls and other gangs as major focal points. The mundane internal affairs consume a greater portion of time than the general public realizes, since only the dramatic captures their attention. This doesn't imply that internal affairs are less stimulating to the gang members; they are only hidden from the ears and eyes of outsiders.

Internal affairs established the pecking order, selective bonding, and loyalty priorities. It seemed strange to me that a member with high status in the pecking order could so easily bond with an underling who was considered to be of little consequence, but it happened.

A case in point: Ralph and Russell. Now, Ralph was brilliant when it came to auto mechanics and man's control over machines. He could take a car apart, modify it, fix it, reassemble it, and make it dance a jig when encouraged to do so. He became our prized getaway driver on a few very critical expeditions. Ralph was, in unwritten terms, a member of the power base.

Russell, on the other hand, was intellectually superior to all of us, but he was shy. He was considered little more than a hanger-on and symbol of our benevolence toward the underdog. The bond between Ralph and Russell included a willingness on Ralph's part to put his reputation on the line to protect the little squirt.

Russell had a job as delivery boy for a florist and thus delivered flowers from wealthy suitors and apologetic misfit husbands to their respective sweethearts. Having a non-aggressive nature and passive stance when faced with animosity, it was common for Russell to be the brunt of fun-seeking intimidators. He was regularly ambushed, and his flowers were destroyed before he could deliver them. Ralph adopted Russell and appointed himself as Russell's savior. Here is one example of what happened.

It was a lazy afternoon and several of us were in our hideout wasting time doing a whole lot of nothing.

"Russell, what's up, buddy?" Ralph asked. "You look down in the mouth. Is someone giving you a bad time?"

"No, it's nothing," Russell answered.

"Come on, old buddy, tell me what's wrong," Ralph insisted.

Russell was reluctant to say anything, but the pressure of several sets of eyes glued on his forehead drew out his tale of woe.

"When's your next delivery?" asked Ralph.

"Now!" responded Russell. "My flower truck's parked in the alley. I'm afraid to go. I know they'll be waiting for me. It happens every Thursday. I think I'm their Thursday entertainment."

"Well, let's not disappoint them," said Ralph as he put his arm around Russell and nearly dragged him into the alley. Ralph pushed Russell into the driver seat and climbed into the back of the van. We watched them leave.

It wasn't until late that night when we, who were still in the hideout, doing a great deal of nothing, received the modestly enthusiastic report from Russell.

"Ralph scared the shit out of me," said Russell. "Those damn buggers came up behind me and bumped my bumper. Ralph was in the aisle between the flower racks, in the back of the van. Ralph came up front, put one hand on the steering wheel, pulled me out of the driver's seat, and slid in behind the wheel. The buggers tried to pass me like they always do. They were going to get in front of me and slow down, make me stop, and then destroy all the flowers.

"When they pulled up next to us, Ralph swerved the van at them. They tried to avoid us and veered head on into traffic coming the other way. They jammed on their brakes and skidded sideways in front of the other cars. There was a lot of squealing of brakes, but no one hit them. Ralph jammed on the brakes too and, like some kind of emperor, strolled back to their car, grabbed the driver by his shirt, said something, came back, and we drove away."

"What'd he say?" I asked.

"I don't know. All he told me was that they wouldn't bother me anymore. He drove the van to his house, got out, and went into his garage. He said he needed to get his Hudson back together."

"That's it?" asked Bruce.

"Yeah, that's it. I went and delivered the flowers and took the van back to the florist."

"Jeez!" exclaimed Bruce. No one else said anything. We just returned to doing nothing.

Internal happenings sometimes fall like dominoes standing on end in a line. This was one of those times. After a few minutes, Bruce announced, "My dad's a smuggler."

"What?" I asked.

"Didn't you know? My dad's a smuggler," he repeated.

Sometimes even outspoken troublemakers like Bruce have an opportunity for recognition from the boys. His claim was kind of doubtful, but plausible.

"What do you mean, a smuggler?" Herman asked.

"He's captain of a barge that takes trains back and forth across the Detroit River from Canada. He smuggles things in oil drums."

"Things, like what?" Herman asked.

"Right now it's tomatoes."

"Tomatoes? You're nuts, nobody smuggles tomatoes." Herman was not about to accept this as viable contraband.

"Sure they do," said Bruce with a degree of confidence not previously exhibited. "During the war my dad smuggled all kind of things. Now he only smuggles tomatoes. Try buying tomatoes and see how hard they are to get and how much you have to pay for them."

Herman was temporarily stumped. Bruce sounded too sure of himself. Herman finally said, "I don't believe it."

"Come on to my house. I'll show you. I'll even treat everyone to tomato and cheese sandwiches." Bruce was not going to be denied his glory in his dad's spotlight, and my boys were tired of doing nothing. Tomato and cheese sandwiches sounded pretty good.

"Do we get some milk too?" asked Dave as we all streamed out of the hideout en route to Bruce's place.

"Beer would be better," added George.

"Who wants to ride with me?" I asked. "I have my brother's Mighty Tin for the day."

To my astonishment, seven energetic louts, two of whom abandoned their own cars, struggled to cram themselves into the Mighty Tin, a Crosley station wagon that I think was designed for four midgets. It took a few minutes, but they accomplished the impossible. There was one small problem: There was no room for me behind the steering wheel. It took another five minutes of pushing, shoving, twisting, and turning before I was able to join my passengers.

"This is really stupid," said Bruce.

"Don't complain, at least you're on top," complained Herman, who was somewhere below the mass of smelly humanity.

"Damn it," blurted George. "Some asshole just bit my leg."

"Yuck, hairy raw meat," moaned James.

"It's so damn hot in here the leg will be cooked in a minute," added Dave. "Then it'll taste better."

I put my arm between the spokes of the steering wheel to twist the key and start the car. Some idiot twisted the steering wheel and nearly broke my arm. Finally, with chattering and quaking, we got under way. Once the bodies settled into a compact mass and the bitching reduced to occasional gripes, we accelerated to twenty miles an hour and I relaxed a little. I didn't want to damage my brother's car. Bruce's place was only three blocks away, so reaching our destination safely was a foregone conclusion.

Once across Gratiot Avenue, we only needed to go five houses in order to enjoy the tomato and cheese sandwiches. The only thing certain in our lives was uncertainly. When I approached the stop sign at Gratiot and applied the brakes, it was a stimulating surprise to continue our forward motion and dash across the four lanes and two sets of streetcar tracks without so much as a hint of slowing down.

In retrospect, I marvel at the Lord's kindness to stupid teenagers. As if by design, we intermingled with cars passing in front and behind us without a scratch, let alone becoming a jelly roll. The guys were so intent on their body rearrangement exercise that they weren't aware of their brush with eternity.

I stopped the Crosley in front of Bruce's home by skidding along the curb and pumping the spongy brake pedal. Everyone fell out, forming a pile on the grass. They sounded like a bunch of giddy girls after their first date.

"That is one small car," said Herman, who had gone from the bottom of the pile in the car to the top of the pile on the grass.

"Get your elbow out of my face," mumbled George.

"How does your brother fit into that tin can?" asked James

"It's not easy, but he likes getting fifty miles to a gallon of gas. He saves a lot of money that way," I said.

"Wow, he's a cheapskate. He probably didn't pay more than two hundred and fifty smackers for it," said Bruce.

"Quit complaining, it got us here, didn't it?" I was getting a little irritated. "Let's see your damn smuggled tomatoes."

This was a proud moment for Bruce. He led the way through the back door and directly to the basement, where he lifted the lid of an oil drum and, from a box wedged inside, withdrew several large, slightly green tomatoes.

"I hate tomatoes," I said.

"Don't be a spoil sport. They're great, and you'll love them with cheese. Everyone, grab two or three and follow me." Bruce climbed the steps, followed by tomato-toting troubadours singing, "Cha Chita Tomato has a rosy view, when she bends down, you can see there's two…"

We made dozens of tomato and cheese sandwiches and gobbled them down with beer and milk chasers.

"These are really good," said Herman.

"Especially since they're free," said Dave.

"No, because they're smuggled," said James.

"I like 'em 'cause I'm hungry," added Jake

"What do you think?" Bruce asked me.

"Sure, they're wonderful. I don't know how I've lived without them for so long," I said.

Dave splattered the table with a mouthful of tomato when he tried not to laugh. Herman wiped some off his face and threw a tomato at Dave, but missed. It careened off the shoulder of James, who returned the favor by jettisoning half a sandwich at Herman. It was certainly a fact of life that one thrown tomato deserves another. The short skirmish ended in drudgery, but not regret. It took a good hour to clean up the mess.

On occasions, when boredom invaded the hideout, intellectual discussions were considered temporarily acceptable. A creative vision was held in high esteem. The topics included girls, stealing, adventure planning, cars, and similar earth shattering subjects. Deliberations often concluded with practical strategies such as:

1. Steal a book from the public library. It must be a novel with an interesting title.
2. Slowly walk away from the crime scene. Running was not acceptable.
3. If really bored, read it.
4. If feeling generous, give it to a friend, otherwise
5. With a razor blade carefully cut out the last chapter of the book.
6. Burn the last chapter.
7. Carefully remove the library pocket from inside the book.
8. Burn the library pocket, and the "return due date" card found in the pocket.
9. Sell the book to someone you don't like.
10. Spend the money.

Most of the internal affairs of my gang were neither visible to the world nor earth-shattering. They mirrored the life of most youth searching for fun and excitement, and were an add-on to making fun of authorities and privileged snobs. It was through these internal experiences that we built life-long bonds of friendship and loyalty. These relationships were the mainstay of our stability in an unstable environment.

EPISODE FOURTEEN

SMASHED

(Age 16) 1950

My boys and I had held several successful Fuzz Ball Buster Days, but my opportunity to use the family car diminished when my dad purchased his first new car, a slick forest-green Oldsmobile. It was a streamlined, two-door power machine that made my family appear to be wealthy.

We were, to some degree, following the pattern of the large, poor black community who lived in the slum sections of Detroit. Their housing was pitiful, their clothing often well-worn hand-me-downs, and their quality of life suppressed by bigotry, minimal income inadequate to support their large families, and doors closed to quality education and prestigious social clubs. They compensated by owning quality cars: Cadillacs, Lincolns, and Oldsmobiles.

I was both proud of our new car and slightly embarrassed by the impression it made, that is, the "affective connotation." Nevertheless, I took great pride is driving the Oldsmobile when I was given the opportunity, which was seldom. Dear Old Dad was very protective of his new treasure. An important need to use my dad's new car was just around the corner.

This very special occasion came uninvited and knocked on my door of opportunity. The daughter of the chief of police of Mt. Clements asked me to be her escort to her high school prom. She was the queen of the ball. I was astonished that she asked me, because she was beautiful and must have had thousands of guys chasing after her. Mt. Clements was a small city to the north of Detroit. I knew where it was but never went there.

Maureen was her name. Both of our mothers were patient roommates at Deaconess Hospital, each having a breast removed and sentenced to a short-term confinement for radiation treatment. For several days, we each visited our mothers some, and each other considerably.

Maureen was slim and shapely with all the right equipment in the right places. She wasn't sway-back, and the size of her rump was equal to width of her shoulders. Not too much sand had drained to the bottom, thus she had a perfect hour glass figure. It was not our custom to date girls taller than ourselves, but on this occasion an exception was demanded. I was convinced that there were some advantages to our height differences, and I was determined to discover what they were.

My bullfrog dad was as impressed as I was, and very willing to let me use the new car to take the chief of police's daughter to her prom. I hate to admit it, but I was a little afraid of this lovely damsel. I arranged for Jake to join us and double date to the prom. He had a new steady girlfriend whose father was Chief Justice of Macomb County.

Dating the daughter of the chief of police and the county legal beagle was like sneaking into the Fuzz Ball chicken coup and paying the farmer a compliment for providing such a juicy meal. I fantasized what it would be like to take a short detour on the way home, park on a dark secluded street, and be caught by the Mt. Clements police, necking.

It's probably good that the fantasy didn't materialize, but what did happen was by far a more challenging nightmare. Initially, the prom was spectacular, with good music, great dancing, and a free food table. There were all kinds of little sandwiches, chunks of cheese, crackers with little sliced up green things on them, slices of watermelon, several kind of dips for chips and celery pieces, and, best of all, a chocolate fountain in which we could coat a strawberry. Just sticking your finger in the fountain and licking it worked pretty well too.

Out trip home didn't start out too well. After spending two hours in a hot room dancing and eating, a cool breeze and a light drizzle greeted us when we left the prom. Goose pimples and shivers joined our party.

"I'll get the car and pick you up at the front door," I said.

"We'll wait inside. Honk twice when you get here," suggested Jake.

I was parked in a lot two blocks away. By the time I reached the car, my shirt was welded to my chest, my pants were dripping like a downspout, and my shoes had become mini-foot-bath tubs. I hated to get the seats of Dad's new car wet, but there was no other option.

I picked up Jake and our dates. "Let's not go home yet," said Maureen.

"Good by me," agreed Jake.

"What'd you want to do?" I asked.

"Let's just ride around and enjoy some music on the radio," suggested Maureen.

I turned on the radio and, after searching several stations, settled for WJR. We listened to Perry Como sing "Prisoner of Love," Nat King Cole sing "For Sentimental Reasons," and other favorites by Frank Sinatra, Dinah Shore, and the Ink Spots.

I can testify that, at the moment of disaster, your life does not flash through your mind like a newsreel at the theater. There was a flashing red light mixed with a glaring white beacon from the front and a blinding white light from the driver's side followed by an instantaneous tinkle of what sounded like coins dropping into a monkey's tin cup. Rain gently soaked my lap as it drizzled through the front window frame.

I looked at my date. Her eyes were as large as bowling balls, and her mouth quivered like a shaken bowl of Jell-O.

"You okay?" I asked.

Maureen nodded her head and whispered, "Yes, I think so."

I twisted my head to peer into the back seat. It was a shock to see half the hood of a car sticking through the back side window. It had a rocket-shaped pointed hood ornament. Jake was pressed tight against the passenger side corner, and I could barely see his date's head on his lap.

"Are you okay?" I asked.

"Yeah, we're both okay," Jake said.

The Fuzz and medical emergency squad materialized instantaneously. Everyone was kind, considerate, and concerned. It was three in the morning by the time we were examined for physical damage. The Fuzz quickly discovered the identity of our dates, and their devotion to duty swelled by a factor of zillions.

The Fuzz Balls kept us company while the girls' fathers were on the way to rescue their daughters. I phoned my dad from a phone booth on the corner. I counted. The phone rang eight times. Dad answered.

"Dad, I'm sorry, but I smashed up the car. A police car hit me head-on. His car is sitting on top of our engine. A drunk lady also smashed into the side of the car. Her hood is sticking inside the back side window. All the windows are gone. Both doors fell off, even the one that wasn't hit. It's totally smashed. They can't even tow it away."

I took a breath. I was winded. "It wasn't my fault, Dad. I had a green light. I was only going ten miles an hour. I didn't have anything bad to drink. It was raining. The pavement was slippery. I'm sorry, Dad. I don't know what to do."

Without hesitation, my dad asked, "Son, is anyone hurt?"

"No, we're all okay, but I don't know what to do."

"Where are you?" he asked.

"Thirteen Mile Road and Van Dyke," I said.

"Keep dry and warm. Richard will come and bring you home."

"Dad, I'm sorry."

"Son, it was only a car," he said. "Richard will be there in about twenty minutes."

We waited. Shock crept out of its hideout, and reality seeped into consciousness. Jake was so shaken that he couldn't hold a match steady enough to light a cig. His date had to hold the match for him.

We'd been very fortunate, but Jake's date was by all accounts the prime benefactor of God's protecting expertise. The back of her head had been resting against the back side window. At a critical moment, Jake's inner eye recognized the approaching bright lights as a death threat from Father Time. Jake reached over, gripped the front of her dress, and pulled her toward himself. Her face was buried in his lap as the hood of the oncoming car smashed through the window and partially extended over her prone body.

My dad's car was the major victim. It could not be driven or towed. The police had a truck come from a lumber company, and using a pallet hoist, they lifted Dad's Oldsmobile onto its flatbed. It was impounded by the police and taken for temporary storage with unclaimed stolen autos.

My steel-rimmed glasses were replaced by a magnifying glass through which I saw new meanings for old perceptions. The word "smashed" had meant several things to me: being full of booze so that the mind floats and the body stumbles, having my physical being pounded by the fist of someone who didn't like me, or being in a terrible accident. The term "smashed" tends to have a serious beginning and ending. This car accident was a smashing experience in which I discovered a positive meaning.

Even though my sixteen years of life didn't pass before my mind's eye in flaming colors, the present and future were painted as a brilliant landscape. Because of my dad's response to the loss of his new car, I realized that the treasures I hold in my heart are determined by the priority values I grow in my mind.

EPISODE FIFTEEN

RELAXATION

(Age 16) 1950

There are thousands of ways to relax, even for relatively poor teenagers living adjacent to the inner city of Detroit. For my family, our favorite evening entertainment was listening to our Philco radio. My dad would light three candles and strategically place them around the living room: one by a plant, another behind a lamp, and the third in front of an old Ansonia clock with a shiny class cover over its face. All three candles created dancing shadows on the walls and ceiling. My three brothers, Richard, Floyd, and Gerald, along with Dad and me, would lie on the floor and listen to "Inner Sanctum Mysteries," with its creepy squeaky door opening followed by mysterious murder stories. Our other favorites were "The Shadow Knows," 'The Invisible Man," and sometimes "The Long Ranger" with his sidekick Tonto.

Not all relaxation includes passively lying prone on the floor or being entertained, but it does need to be enjoyable. Pleasure is often enhanced proportionately by the effort required to set favorable conditions. One such experience took place at my Aunt Edna's summer cottage.

The preliminary effort, prior to the Fourth of July, was the annual trip my boys and I took to Ohio to purchase fireworks. These were illegal in Michigan, and the Fuzz waited for us to cross the county line and confiscate our purchases. We hid two small bags under the spare tire that the Fuzz joyously found but missed the mother-lode stashed inside the door panels. We faked dismay until we were on our way.

We didn't use all the fireworks on the Fourth of July. We saved seven depth chargers for use later. These were half-inch-long tubes with the firing wick sticking out the side rather than the end. Their unique feature, which most people didn't know, is that they would continue to burn and explode when dropped in the water. We wisely surmised that saving a few would come in handy at an opportune time in the future.

During the summer, Aunt Edna's cottage was a bee's hive of activity, but was only used on weekends in September. It seemed to me that a midweek party at the cottage would be a perfect way to conclude the use of the cottage for the year. My mom and dad had a key to the cottage, which they hid in the kitchen cupboard under a stack of coffee cup saucers. I knew because I was observant. I also knew it would be wrong to take the key, but I took it anyhow. From that moment to this very day, more than fifty years later, I have been hounded by guilt, and that is only a quarter of the price I've had to pay.

Our trip to the cottage was a sign that this was not going to be the perfect caper. On a very busy highway, Ralph's car made unlikely friends with a nail. The shoulder was very narrow, and changing the tire was dangerous. We didn't have a flare, orange road cone, or reflector to warn the fast-approaching traffic. James, our tall basketball center, improvised by waving his sweetheart's red bathing suit at the oncoming motorists. He almost got creamed a couple of times.

Ten miles farther down the road, Bruce, our second driver, ran out of gas. Later, just prior to reaching Cedar Island Lake, we stopped at the Round Lake Grocery Store for beer and party foods. Ten of us collectively, after chipping in to pay for Bruce's gasoline, didn't have enough money to pay for what we selected. To make things worse, Bruce and Ron argued over what we would put back on the shelf. When Ralph tried to calm their tempers, he got punched in the eye, fell backward, and broke two bottles of wine in a rack that he knocked over. After paying for the wine, we left with a few bags of chips and one six-pack of beer.

"Cheer up," I said. "Edna's probably got some food in the fridge."

"Probably cheese," offered Bruce.

"Probably cottage cheese," added Ron.

"Probably moldy cottage cheese," said James.

Our companions, four lovely ladies, simply giggled. They weren't interested in eating food anyhow, especially cheese.

"Okay, when we get there, let's keep the noise down. The neighbors know me, and I don't want to draw any more attention than necessary," I said.

"Sure, we'll be quiet, just like little mice eating moldy cottage cheese," said Herman.

It was useless. *No one is going to listen to me. A leader of a gang should have more control than this. Maybe fear and intimidation is a better way to manage this bunch of bananas. I wish I hadn't taken the key and come to the cottage. I'm really going to catch hell for this.*

It was too late to retreat. Forward was the only direction I could go. We drove the last three miles to Cedar Island Lake. To my relief, none of the neighboring cottages were occupied. Midweek September was wind-down time. One neighbor had already boarded up the windows for the winter. We immediately headed to the lake; the cottage could wait.

I brought the depth chargers for our party outing. We were not animal rights activists, so what I planned to do was within our creed of justice.

In Cedar Island Lake, there were hundreds of small fish that made their nests close to the shoreline. With their tails they created small holes lined with stones and laid eggs in the holes. They swam over their eggs and chased away intruders. Their major enemy was the water moccasin, who, with mouth open, casually swam into the "no enter zone" of a guarding mother fish. The mother fish would dash at the intruder and become the snakes' lunch.

We were disappointed. We found no fish along the shoreline. Evidently we were out of sync with their mating cycle. Fortunately, a couple of water moccasins were lolling around, probably hoping a careless fish would stray past and provide an afternoon snack. We found it relaxing to sit on the breakwater, tie a stone to a depth charger, light it, and drop it in the water in front of a water moccasin. They didn't understand that a free lunch wasn't worth losing your head over.

After the demise of two snakes, we placed the remaining five depth chargers, one at a time, under a tin can that my Uncle Ted used to bail out water in an old rowboat. Four times it shot skyward about thirty feet. The fifth time, the sides split open and the tin can careened sideways and splashed to its grave fifteen feet off shore.

"Let's eat," suggested Ron.

Upon entering the cottage, we discovered that there wasn't any food in the refrigerator. It was unplugged, and the door blocked open. The electricity didn't work, so we couldn't play the radio. There was no wood, so we couldn't light a fire in the potbelly stove, and there were no sheets or blankets on the day bed.

"I'll check upstairs to see if I can find some blankets so we can keep warm," said Herman.

"Great party, Labuhn," remarked Bruce.

"Leave any time you want. I'll keep Barb company," said Ron.

"Not if I can help it," said Barb. She wasn't about to be passed around like a basketball.

Herman nearly fell down the stairs. "Damn narrow steps. Stupid things are made for baby feet. There's nothing up there but three double beds and one single."

"That sounds good to me," said Ralph. His girl Shirley studied her feet, and a tinge of pink flushed her face.

"Yeah," drawled out James. Marlene squeezed his arm, and the left edge of her mouth twitched.

"There are no sheets or blankets up there either," added Herman.

"We'll just have to keep each other warm, I guess." Bruce was beginning to like the party.

Bruce and Barb, James and Marlene, Ralph and Shirley, and Herman and Marilyn seemed to merge into each other's arms like cats in heat, purring. The Fourth of July fireworks were dull compared to the lights that were flashing between them. *I wonder who's going to get stuck with the single bed? Probably Herman and Marilyn. It's logical since he's the biggest.*

"There aren't any walls between the beds either," said Herman.

The world stood still for about twenty seconds before Ron broke into laughter that would have made Clem Kadiddle Hopper proud.

I said, "Shame on you, Ron, you're a mean widdle kid."

It only took another five seconds for everyone except Ralph to join in the merriment. Ralph's life centered around repairing, driving, and wrecking cars at the Detroit City Motor Speedway. He had not become acquainted with Red Skelton's crazy humor.

Bruce, with Barb in tow, dashed up the steps, which started a stampede. In less than fifteen seconds, only Ron and I were left on the main floor.

"Keep your hands to yourself," said Ron.

"You really are a mean widdle kid," I said. We were relaxed and enjoying ourselves immensely.

There was considerable commotion, bordering on rebellion upstairs. Ron and I pieced together enough words to decipher the problem. Herman got stuck with the single bed and was not one bit happy.

"Is it true that there are no walls up there?" asked Ron.

"Yep," I said, "but there are two wires that criss-cross the room. They have curtains that go between the beds."

"They'll never find them. They only have one thing in mind," said Ron.

"Yeah, I know. Even if they do, it will only block the vision, not the groans and moans."

Ron asked, "Did you ever hear a hormone?"

"No, and I've never seen one either," I said. After a few moments of silly laughter, I added, "Let's go sit on the dock for a while."

Ron and I walked down to the dock, but there wasn't any dock. It had been hauled out of the water and stored for the winter. We sat on the breakwater for about three minutes and were so cold that we went back up to the cottage. It was relatively quiet when we returned. There was minimal creaking and squeaking intermingled with an occasional giggle.

We rummaged around and found a stack of sheets and blankets in a box under the stairs.

"You want to take some upstairs for our guests?" I asked.

"Not me!" said Ron. "I'd like to live another day."

"At least we'll keep warm. You take one end of the day bed. I'll take the other."

We settled down and after a few minutes dozed off. When I woke up, there was dead silence in the cottage. I thought, *One of the greatest joys of relaxing must come after a major expenditure of sweat-producing activity.*

About one in the morning, Herman and Marilyn came down. The only thing Herman had to say was, "Damn bed is as small as the steps."

"Sure is dark in here. Herman, turn on the lights so I can use the bathroom," said Marilyn.

"Sorry, honey. There's no electricity and no water in the potty."

"Oh, shit."

"You got that right," Ron added with a slight chuckle.

By one-thirty, the whole crew assembled in the main room, which included a dining table, four chairs, the potbelly stove, the day bed, and a dresser used for storing cards, dice, board games, tablecloths, and other miscellaneous items.

A small L cove housed the kitchen, and a closet-sized room had a toilet and a sink. Bruce came out of the bathroom and announced, "The toilet doesn't work, and there's no toilet paper."

Ron asked, "What'd you use, your hanky?"

Bruce threw a punch at Ron, who ducked and crashed into the potbelly stove. The stove pipe came apart at the base and disconnected from the ceiling. It crashed down onto the daybed, spilling soot all over the bed and floor.

My boys did the best they could to clean up the mess. There wasn't any water in the tap, so Ralph soaked a table cloth in the lake. He tried to clean up the soot, but only smeared it into the day bed mattress and made graphic streaks all over the floor.

"I think we better go before things get any worse," suggested Ron.

"Let's go. Party's over," I announced.

After everyone was out of the cottage and in their cars, I was about to lock the door when Ron suggested, "I'd leave it unlocked, if I were you. It'll look like vandals have been in there."

"But Uncle Ted always locks it," I said.

"He forgot the last time he was here," Ron stated.

"Yeah, you're right!"

The trip back to Detroit was quick and quiet, with everyone but the drivers snuggling and snoozing. At home, I easily slipped into the house, replaced the cottage key under the stack of saucers, and climbed into bed without disturbing a soul. It had been fun and relaxing for some, but my soul was so disturbed that sleep didn't come easily. I had done wrong, knew it, and wished there was some way I could undo the whole excursion. Like tooth paste, once it's out of the tube, it's impossible to put it back in.

EPISODE SIXTEEN

COWBOYS AND INDIANS

(Age 17) 1951

The four seasons bring dramatic changes to the streets of Detroit. Fall is a wonderful relief after a dry spell of ninety-degree summer. The colors and sounds are invigorating as well. Large black clouds move in, lightning dances in jagged streaks and brilliant flashes, booming thunder vibrates the window panes, marble-size balls of water beat down like machine gun fire. Water swirls along the gutter, turning oil drippings from cars into rainbow colors on the asphalt, and the torrent mixed with cigarette butts, condoms, and colorful candy wrappers dashes through steel grates built into the curb, cascading downward into the sewers. It's beautiful.

Relief from summer comes in many forms. For my boys, a highlight was an annual visit to the country, to the nearest state park. In the fall, these pristine lands are protected by the park rangers. They draped a steel chain across the entrance and put a "Closed for the season" sign over the "Pay here for camp sites" sign that was screwed on the one main entrance booth.

We drove our cars around the steel post at the edge of the roadway on the well-worn tracks of previous trespassers. It wasn't much trouble, but it did get mud on our tires, as well as the fender skirts.

This was planned as a two-day outing, so we came well-stocked with beer, toilet paper, and Boy Scout hatchets to chop down small trees for fire wood. Hot dogs, buns, catsup, mustard, pickle relish, chips, marshmallows, and Twinkies for desert were the planned menu. It was great being out in the Wild West of Detroit with the comfort of our cars for sleeping, although we didn't expect to get much sleep.

I led the parade into the park, driving my dad's forest-green 1949 Nash Ambassador, which is considered an upside-down bathtub. Despite its funny reputation, it was the first car with a one-piece curved windshield and seats that folded down into an uncomfortable bed. There were fourteen of us in six cars, so the sleeping arrangements would be a little tight. Thus the Nash was viewed as a prize for the night.

After passing the entrance booth, I stopped the parade to impart wise advice to my boys. Ralph driving his low-slung streamline 1948 Hudson, known as the first step-down-into car, nearly crashed into me.

"What the hell did you stop for, idiot? You nearly got my car wrecked."

"Gripe, gripe, gripe," I said. "If you hadn't stopped, it'd have been your own fault, stupid. Besides, you love wrecking cars. You do it every week at the speedway demolition derby."

"Yeah, but not my own car." Ralph,, usually cool-headed, was agitated for some reason. Bruce, from car three, interrupted our confrontation. Bruce drove a 1940 dark blue DeSoto, the first car I knew of that had fluid drive. It wasn't fast, but it was smooth.

"What's going on? You guys lost already?"

"Shut up, pipsqueak, or I'll clean your clock." Ralph,'s face didn't show any anger.

"Yeah, shut up," I said. "We're just considering what kind of campsite we need."

"Okay, I get it. Don't get your dander up."

It was unusual for Bruce to back down so quickly. Ralph, was evidently having fun, and my little white lie must have confused Bruce. James, from car four, a gray Plymouth with no special features to enhance its existence, casually strode up. Because of his long legs, he arrived before George in car five opened his car door. George drove a 1941 Ford coupe, which was the most popular car among teenagers at the time. It was fast, reaching 60 miles per hour in a quarter of a mile.

The last to arrive for my words of wisdom was Dave, whose car was a 1942 hand-painted yellow Chevy wreck. Three fenders were badly dented and the fourth was missing. The passenger side window was also missing, and a piece of foggy plastic was taped over the opening to keep bugs out. How he saw anything through the shattered front window only God knows.

Dave asked, "What's the convention for?"

"Ask the master mind, he's got all the answers." Ralph,'s dry humor was running on high octane.

"Okay, guys. I just wanted to make sure everyone understands the need to move slowly, with our headlights off and our horns silent. We don't want the park rangers to know we're here. Everyone agree?"

"Sure, why not," said James.

Everyone gave tacit approval, returned to their cars, and we started our slow drive into the dark of the park. In less than twenty feet, dear Ralph punched one sharp beep on his horn. He was obviously still irritated at my abruptly stopping in front of him.

In another twenty feet, Bruce gave two short beeps. In unison, Dave and James pressed hard and long on their horns. Ralph, flashed his headlights one short blast, which he accompanied with blowing "Hail, Hail, the Gang's all Here" on his musical horn. Not to be outdone, George turned on his headlights and trumpeted his existence by blowing a Model T ooogah horn he had installed in his Ford. Russell, my front seat passenger, reached over and blew the horn.

Oh, what the hell! I turned on my headlights and tromped on the gas. By the time we reached the campground, we were traveling 45 miles per hour. *So much for a slow, quite, dark, and inconspicuous entrance*, I thought.

There was a lot of laughing and gaiety as the happy campers scrambled from their cars. With hatchets in hand, we tackled the nearest trees for fire wood and within a half an hour had enough wood to last long enough to cook our hot dogs and roast some marshmallows over the dying embers.

The first glitch of our expedition set off a chain reaction resulting in an Indian versus settler war. Dave, in his typical naïve manner, tried to cut down a tree too big for our immediate needs and was still working on it after the rest of us had ceased from our labor.

"Dave," yelled Bruce.

Dave looked up, and Bruce, with an Indian whoop, threw his hatchet at him. Dave retaliated by throwing his hatchet at Bruce, who was a settler, seated in the middle of the pack. Everyone scattered, and within a split-hair of a second, hatchets were flying in all directions. It was hard to tell who were Indians and who were settlers. Russell, the wimp, was a true settler. He escaped and hid on the floor in the back seat of my Nash.

The war lasted a half-hour. It was prolonged because several aspiring Indians couldn't find their hatchets in the woods, and one Indian fell into the creek. Herman was the only casualty. On his head he had a four-inch gash surrounded by scrape marks. Knocking on wood had a new meaning as his frail head lost the battle with a thick tree branch. Herman didn't appreciate still having a head of hair after dodging a flying hatchet.

After the Indian war, we embarked on dinner and encountered a second glitch in our expedition. We forgot to bring hot dog buns and catsup.

"No big deal. We're roughing it. Just put the hot dog on a stick, dab it with mustard, and eat it off the stick," advised Bruce.

"What about the pickle relish?" asked Dave.

"Just put it in your hand and dip the dog in it," said Bruce.

"Oh," responded Dave. "I guess that'll work."

"What a dip," mumbled Bruce, just audible enough for me to hear.

Glitch three couldn't have happened to a better person. Bruce burned his lip by biting into a red-hot spark at the bottom of his first dog. He howled like a wounded coyote.

Dave said, "Eat a little pickle relish. It's cool stuff. You'll feel better."

Capping off the evening, we played cowboys, sitting around our campfire singing old favorites. We started with "John Jacob Jingle Heimer Schmidt," followed by our version of "My Bonny."

"My bonny has tuberculosis
My bonny has only one lung
My bonny spits blood in a bucket
And dries it and chews it for gum.

"Bring back, Oh, bring back

Oh, bring back my bucket
To me, to me. Bring back…"

We then sang the Chinaman song, mostly because we loved the refrain Chick-a-cha-luke-cha-luke-cha-pan-aloppy-aloppy-chick-a-cha-loloppy-chick-a-cha-luke-cha-luke-cha-pan-aloppy-aloppy-china-man.

The final glitch of our expedition into the wild woods was a sudden rainstorm that sent us dashing to our cars and extinguished our campfire. It lasted a whole ten minutes and dampened our spirits. No one was willing to cut down wet green trees or rekindle the campfire.

We huddled in our cold cars, drinking beer and eating chips, marshmallows, and Twinkies. By five the next morning, there were complaints of aches and pains from sleeping across split front seats, being folded up like safety pins to fit between the doors, or stretched over humps in the seats that didn't correspond to the contour of our bodies. My gang was a speedy bunch. Our planned two-day outing in the woods was completed in one day. We looked forward to bragging to our friends about the wonderful time we had in the country. Next year will be great fun, too.

EPISODE SEVENTEEN

COPS & ROBBERS

(Age 17) 1951

"What-cha got?"

"It's a peapod. I swiped it from Mike's pool hall," answered Russell.

"Really? Lordy, help us. I've never seen you swipe anything."

Russell was so straight-laced that one time he spent an hour looking for the unfortunate soul who had lost a quarter he'd found.

"It looks like an awfully small pot to pee in," said James, as he examined the five-inch-high red plastic milk-bottle-shaped vessel.

"You don't pee in it," responded Russell. "It's got peas in it. Here, let me show you." All the guys gathered around to see Russell's borrowed treasure. He shook the peapod and it rattled. He turned it over and dumped several small white plastic balls into his hands, each having one flat side embossed with a black number.

"These are the peas. There are fifteen of them, each one with a pool ball number printed on it. You put all the peas in the peapod, shake it, and each pool player takes out one pea."

Russell had everyone's attention.

"The number on the pea is your pool ball number. You don't let anyone see or know what number you have."

"What then?" asked Bruce.

Russell was enjoying the attention and opportunity to be a teacher. "You play a game of pool. Everyone shoots at any ball they feel like, except the ball with their number on it. If someone shoots your ball into a pocket, you're out of the game."

"How do you win?" asked George.

"The game is over when only one person still has his pool ball on the table. He's the winner."

It was no surprise that the boys liked new games and quickly initiated their first peapod pool contest. Unfortunately, when the first few players were eliminated from the game, they made it difficult for the few who still had a chance to win. They took balls off the table, bumped cue sticks when a player was about to take a shot, and used the side cushion as a line to toss pennies. The pressure to control internal mob violence dictated the need for a diversion.

The timing and setting were perfect to implement another new event. Twelve cars were lined up behind our hideout, on one side of the alley, crammed against the garbage cans to allow enough space for others to squeeze their way past. Seldom did all my boys have use of a car at the same time, thus it was deemed necessary that I take advantage of this good fortune. The Fuzz Balls were a secondary concern on my mind.

Our monopoly of the alley was an invitation for the neighbors to complain to the Fuzz and have them raid our den. The Fuzz would certainly interrogate us, probably search our place for stolen contraband and booze, and might even write a few tickets for disturbing the peace or cluttering the alley. Hell, clutter is what alleys were made to accommodate.

"Hey, guys, calm it down, will ya?" I shouted to get their attention.

Twelve loudmouths cramped in a two-car garage trying to play pool, hammering a stupid ditty on the out-of-tune piano, or simply guzzling beer is not a recipe for orderly conduct. It is more like a one-ring circus with only the clowns and the ringmaster. No one knew or cared that the tent smelled like stale elephant pancakes.

"Hey, guys, calm it down, will ya?"

"Hey, guys, calm it down."

"Damn it, calm it down. The Fuzz want it quiet in here," I shouted.

That did it. Silence descended like a guillotine chopping blade. Bruce dashed to the door and looked out to see if the Fuzz had us surrounded.

"That's more like it," I said quietly.

"There's no damn Fuzz out there," said Bruce.

"I know," I said. "I need everyone's attention. We have twelve cars tonight. It's a good time to play cops and robbers."

No one knew what I was talking about. As children, we had played cops and robbers. It was our version of playing hide-and-seek. We chose up sides, the robbers hid, and the cops tried to find and shoot them with water pistols. Putting water with red cake frosting dye in the squirt gun gave proof of making a kill. The robbers had the advantage, as from their hiding place they could shoot the cops before the cops knew they were within range.

"That's dumb," said George. "Only little kids play cops and robbers."

"Not with cars," I said.

It's amazing how such a simple idea can silence an unruly audience. As I expected, Bruce, with his usual obnoxious manner, shot the first round of bullets at my idea. "How the hell are the robbers going to hide their cars? How are the cops going to shoot the robbers? How are we going to know who the hell is who in the dark? It is dark outside you know!"

I was prepared for his tirade. "We're not going to hide the cars or shoot each other. We don't need any damn red cake dye either."

Bruce retaliated, "Don't be so touchy. I only want to know what you're talking about."

"Shut your yap, will ya?" interjected Herman.

"Cool it, stupid," added George.

"Up your—" responded Bruce as pandemonium erupted and Jake threw a beer bottle at him.

"Quiet!" I shouted. "Save your shit slinging for—"

A second beer bottle flung by Dave crashed through a twelve-by-twelve-inch window in the alley garage door. It would have been nice if calm had returned at my beck and call. It didn't, but the shattering of glass silenced the masses.

"That'll cost you, Dave," I said. "You pay for and repair the window."

No one spoke.

"Here is what I have in mind," I said, changing the focus back to my cops and robbers idea. The more an idea could be challenged, the greater the interest in pursuing ways to accomplish its ridiculous conclusions. I boldly laid out details of how the game would be played.

"We'll draw straws and choose up teams. There will be two cop cars for every robber car. The robbers get a three-minute head start. They can drive anywhere they want within our Denby High turf. The cops then try to find and catch the robbers."

"Great!" said Bruce, who never seemed phased by hostility toward him, or sidetracked from pushing his nerve-shattering opinions. He was like the ant that crawled up the elephant's leg with the intention of rape: often biting off more than he could screw. With his big mouth, he often injected nonessential issues that didn't deserve consideration. He did raise one pregnant detail. "Just how do the cops catch a robber?"

"Easy," volunteered Russell, our insightful gang geek. "A robber is caught when one Fuzz car is against the front bumper and another is against the rear bumper of a robber's car."

Bruce's mouth fell open in disbelief. "Easy? Yeah! Sure, at twenty or thirty miles an hour? I don't want my dad's car squashed between two dumb ass cop cars. You guys are crazy. Let's just relax and enjoy a game of pool, or get some girls to come over."

"Spoil sport," said Jake.

"El-chick-e-own," added Ron.

"You'd have a better chance of catching a cold in the desert than a robber in a stalled car in the alley," jibed Dave.

"Enough, enough." I brought the debate, if that's what it was, to a screeching halt, and in my usual fashion again changed the focus. "Someone make some straws so we can get the game on the road."

Without hesitation, Russell took the peapod from the pool table and suggested, "Everyone can draw a pea from the peapod. There are twelve of us with cars. The four with the lowest numbers will be robbers and the rest will be the cops. Bruce, you draw first."

"Why me? I don't even want to play the stupid game."

Russell was a savvy opponent. "Bruce, you draw first. That way you have the greatest opportunity to be a cop and not get your dad's car smashed by plowing into the front or back of a robber."

"What if I get a low number and need to be a robber?" Bruce asked.

Russell was up to the challenge. "I suggest that you negotiate with a cop and strike a compromise. For a small remuneration, you trade a robber pea for a cop's pea. That way you get what you want."

"What's a remuneration?" asked Bruce.

"It's like a bribe," said George. "You pay someone, like a dollar, to change peas. You become a cop and he becomes a robber."

"What if no one will trade their pea with me?" Bruce asked.

"For a buck, I'll do it," said Dave.

"Me too," added George.

"Okay, okay. Give me the damn peapod." Bruce shook the peapod and dumped out a pea in his hand. It was number thirteen, thus a cop winner. "Is today Friday?" he asked.

"No, it's not Friday, there are no black cats to cross your path, and praise the Lord, you didn't get the black eight ball. You're home free," said Russell. "Pass the peapod around."

Bruce handed the peapod to George who shook out a pea and passed the peapod on to James. The peapod made the rounds. A damn, shit, and hell expletive pierced the near silence as James, Jake, and Tom drew low numbers. Unfortunately, I drew a low number too. It was interesting that among our clan of petty thieves no one wanted to a robber.

"Let's hit the road, guys, before the Fuzz bust us for loitering," I said.

Once in the alley, I gave the robbers last-minute instructions. "Listen, we don't want to damage our dads' cars, so if it looks like we're going to get trapped between two cop cars, just stop and let them catch you. Remember, it's just a game."

"Good idea. They won't know we'll give up that easy, so they'll be afraid to approach a demolition derby robber," agreed James.

"Especially Bruce," chuckled Tom.

We gunned our engines and laid a streak of rubber in the alley as we sped away. It was an interesting night, with only one casualty: Me! I turned into the Grover street alley and raced toward the other end. In the rearview mirror, headlights appeared. *Darn, spotted already.*

I jammed on the brakes, jumped out, ran to the two nearest oil drum garbage cans behind my dad's car, and dumped them over in the middle of the alley. I jumped back in the car and sped towards the other end of the alley. Headlights appeared in front of me. *Almost trapped, but not quite.*

I passed a vacant lot on the driver's side, continued one house length, jammed on the brakes again, jumped out of the car, ran to the nearest oil drum garbage cans in front of my car, and dumped two of them over in the center of the alley.

Squealing wheels in reverse, I backed up past the vacant lot again. The car behind me had stopped, removed the dumped-over garbage cans, and was again moving in my direction. I floored the gas pedal, swerved into the vacant lot, and headed for freedom of the open street. *I'll be safe in seconds,* I thought.

Before I was able to achieve any real momentum, my dad's car crashed through the roof of a wood-, cardboard-, and dirt-covered hideout hole dug by some local twerps in the center of the vacant lot.

Dave, the first cop to arrive, inquired, "You okay?"

"Yeah! just fine. I intentionally drove my dad's car into that hole."

Later that night, my boys helped me dig out the car. "Thanks, guys. I'll see ya tomorrow." *How am I going to explain the missing grill and dented fender? Vandals? That'll never work. Tell the truth? That'll never work. Maybe half the truth. That's it. I took a shortcut home through a vacant lot and drove into a kid's club house, a hole in the ground covered with cardboard and dirt.*

EPISODE EIGHTEEN

THE TWO STEP

(Age 18) 1952

Arthur Murray became famous with his "magic two step." It could be mastered in less than a minute, and with this knowledge, you could traverse the dance floor in every direction with anyone. Having my own gang and a bodyguard didn't mean that I was lacking in culture. I didn't believe I had *much* culture, but as part of my social life I was a member of the Edwin Denby High School Dance Club.

Unfortunately, my fame as a dancer came at the expense of a major embarrassment. The club was scheduled for a synchronized dance performance at a general assembly of Denby High's student body. In order to fully appreciate my innocence in this performance, it is necessary for you to understand the mitigating circumstances.

The auditorium stage had two large trapdoors in the floor that opened into a basement where scenery, props, and other theatrical paraphernalia were stored when not in use. Lying horizontal with the stage floor, hinged steel rings were nestled in pockets large enough for two hands to reach in, grab the rings, pull up, and open the trapdoors.

Our dance routine was a waltz performed by eight couples who, at the start, were arranged in a semi-circle. My partner was June, a rather busty beauty. The grand curtain was drawn open. The couples on each end of the semi-circle glided away from the end, and after two measures the next couple followed in their footsteps. June and I were in the last set to swing into the pattern established by the leaders.

In a waltz, it's important to balance on the balls of your feet and slide each foot forward smoothly. With my first step, toe down, heel up, leaning slightly forward to lead my partner, I gracefully slid my foot into a pocket and under the steel ring in the trap door. June fell backward. I fell forward and I bounced off her busts like a basketball dribbled by a pro. Our routine was an instant success with the students and promoted the dance club, though our instructor wasn't impressed.

Later that day, back in our hideout, the boys were profuse with their praise of my dance performance. Herman's praise was more like a pat on the back with a sword than the tongue-in-cheek humor he intended. "That was a great performance. You made us feel proud to be members of Club AFO."

"I thought June's expression, when you fell on her, was an invitation to go dancing in her bedroom," said James.

There were several more vivid comments made that I ignored. Because of my newfound fame as a dancer, several fe-lions sought my partnership for the Senior Prom. I chose Marlene, a beautiful, slightly shy, and less aggressive junior. I had danced with her at one of the school's bi-monthly dance socials and was aware that she was not a very good dancer. I liked her a lot.

My AFO boys and I had never worn tuxedos, and we wanted to do this party up right. We ordered white tuxedo coats with black pants that sported a silky stripe down the outside of each leg. We all purchased matching red boutonnieres for ourselves and wrist corsages for our dates. We were the lion's roar.

Ron and his date, Charlene, rode with Marlene and me. When we arrived at the Riverside Civic Center, Ron said, "We're early, let's cruise a bit."

We did. Woodward Avenue was our favorite route when cruising for girls or showing off a new car, so we drove that way. When we passed the J.L. Hudson's Department store, Ron asked, "Did you know that Hudson's is the tallest department store in the world?"

"Really?" said Marlene.

"Yup, and they sponsored the first nationally recognized Thanksgiving parade in 1924."

"I don't believe it," I said. "Macy's was the first to have a big Thanksgiving parade."

"No they weren't. Hudson's was. Macy's first parade was two years later. I know 'cause I read it in 'Believe it or Not by Ripley.' Hudson's also has the largest flag in the world. It's fifty feet high and seventy-five feet long. They hang it on the side of the building every Thanksgiving."

"I'll bet you read that in the paper too." I was a little peeved. I didn't like being told I was wrong in front of my date.

"You better believe it, Ripley knows," said Ron.

"Have you ever been to the top of the Penobscot building?" he asked.

"No, have you?" Charlene asked.

"I sure have. When it was built, it was the tallest building in America. The Empire State building was built later, two years later, I think."

I put my mouth in gear before my brain and sarcasm crunched out. "Ron, I didn't know you could read."

Conversation came to a halt. I didn't need a reprimand to realize that no one approved of my sarcastic remark.

"Sorry, Ron. I didn't mean to be nasty."

"Ah, it's okay. I was just showing off for the girls anyhow."

We laughed at Ron's acceptance of my apology and his candor. We drove for a few minutes in silence when, with an obvious deep-seated emotion, Ron said, "I wonder how Dave is doing."

"Who is Dave?" asked Charlene.

After another moment of silence, I explained, "Dave is one of our AFO boys. He should be graduating with us, but he dropped out of school to work. He's got a lot of brothers and sisters, and they need the money real bad."

"Oh," said Charlene. "I'm sorry. It's sad. I know several girls who were expelled because they had babies. Some were even expelled when they were infant-ticipating."

"I know a couple of guys who dropped out to work and take care of their girls and babies," said Ron. "Now they'll probably be stuck in this damn city for life."

"Maybe not. They can climb out of this hole if they try hard enough," said Marlene.

"I know a guy who was kicked out of school for being in a gang, and a girl who killed herself because her boyfriend beat her up. I think we've lost about 100 students from our graduating class," I said.

"Yeah, we're down to about 942 students," Ron reflected, than added, "We'd have even less if some of the guys owned up to fatherhood and supported the gals they'd knocked up."

This conversation was putting a damper on our emotional high for the prom. In silence, we worked our way back to the Riverside Civic Center and the Veterans Memorial building, which was part of the city's master plan for rejuvenation of the riverfront.

The VA Memorial building was beautiful: faced in white marble, located in a park-like setting of trees, gardens, and walkways. Our prom was in one of the ballrooms, decorated with crystal chandeliers and walls draped with maroon curtains.

The prom was spectacular. It seemed like all the students, teachers, and parent chaperones were on the dance floor at the same time. It was like a Ford factory traffic jam at closing time, only the collisions were softer and more inspiring.

Even though Marlene was not the world's best dancer, Arthur Murray's magic two step came to our rescue. Within minutes, we weaved our way through the maze of smooching dancers. I leaned slightly forward, left foot forward, right foot forward, left foot up to right foot, side step to the left, side step to the left again, and repeat. With a slight turn on any of the steps, forward or sideways, we smoothly glided in any direction I wanted to go.

After the prom, we hop-scotched to several parties. Some of the boys slept with their dates after plying them with relaxing potions, mostly beer. Four of us, Herman—who was formally engaged to Marilyn—Ron, Ralph, and I returned our dates to their homes about four in the morning. The prom, our first dance of the night, ended with sighs of satisfaction.

We were high on excitement and sought an encore. I parked my car in a shopping center lot, and Ron and I joined Herman and Ralph in Ralph's car. We cruised Woodward Avenue for a while, but found no action worthy of our attention.

"What d'ya say we go drive on the new freeway?" suggested Herman

"I didn't know it was open yet," I said.

"It's not."

"Well, in that case, let's go drive on the new freeway," I said.

"Did you know that the Detroit freeways are the only ones in the world that are being built below ground level?" asked Ron.

"What?" asked Herman.

"What're ya talking about?" asked Ralph.

"Forget it," I said. "He's been reading Ripley and just wants to show off his superior knowledge."

Ron and I laughed. Herman and Ralph just looked at each other, wondering what hidden message they were missing.

This jaunt on the closed freeway turned out to be our second dance for the night, and the most dangerous activity we'd ever engaged in. Ralph drove around the entrance barriers, and we entered the unlighted freeway. There were trucks, piles of stones and dirt, bulldozers, ditches, piles of steel railings, and concrete drainage tubes scattered everywhere. It was a wonderful obstacle course.

Ralph, who on weekends raced junkers at the Detroit Motor City Speedway, asked, "What d'ya say we see how fast we can go in this jalopy?" He was our car expert and getaway driver when we needed to exit a site in a hurry.

"Sure, why not?" agreed Ron.

I wasn't very happy about the prospects, but I wasn't up to being the chicken spoil sport, so I kept my mouth shut. Dancing our car through the obstacle course was one thing, but Ralph pulled out the throttle for maximum speed, pushed the driver's seat back to its fullest position, removed his shoes, and commenced to steer with his feet. It was a wild jitter-bug dance with death. I thought someone shit in their pants because the car's interior reeked with fear.

"I'd like to go home now," said Ron. "I've had enough for the night."

Ralph just laughed and squeaked his way around a ramp barrier to return us to a paved city street. This was our Detroit style Texas two-step.

EPISODE NINETEEN

TOGETHER SEPARATELY

(Age 18) 1952

It was gone, defunct, kaput. The dance was over, the jig was finished. We had two-stepped our youth away with one foot in our mouth and the other in someone else's pocket. Half of the time we didn't know where one foot was or what the other was doing. We jogged along as though there was no end to roaming the streets and finding interesting things to investigate or confiscate.

Initially, our graduating ceremony speaker captured our attention by telling us that we were all thumbs. He didn't mean green thumbs for making plants grow, or brown thumbs for having plants die when we looked at them. He was talking about the type of people we were.

The speaker told us that all types of people can be represented on the left hand. For example the first finger next to the thumb is the pointer. It points: it's his fault, she did it, let him do it, it's their problem. These are not nice people. They like to blame others and do as little as possible.

The next finger is the tallest one. These people always stand out in the crowd: loud mouth, often pushy, want to make decisions, and are usually control freaks. These are generally not nice people either.

Next comes the finger with the wedding ring. This guy wears the crown of glory. He's the honored guest, either seeking to be recognized as important or actually important by what he says or has already accomplished. This guy is quick to take credit when praise is handed out. These are sometimes nice people, but often tend to be glory mongers.

The last finger is the little guy. He never says much, is seldom helpful, takes up space, doesn't do or accomplish much, and seldom volunteers to do anything. This is a wasted life: a person that neither good nor bad, just a space filler.

Then comes us, graduating class of 1952, a big bunch of thumbs. You notice the thumb is not particularly beautiful, and sometimes it doesn't even go the same direction everyone else is going. What is unique about thumbs is that they are the only ones who can work with all the rest. Try it, the speaker says. We do and he is right. The thumb is the only one that can touch the tip of all the other fingers. It was so good to know that we have the ability to work with all the accusing, big-mouth, glory-seeking, and unimportant people of the world.

My boys and I pretended to listen intently to the rest our graduation ceremony speaker's gems of deportment. He told us about the glorious future that was anxiously waiting to scoop us up in its tiger teeth and spew us into a mansion of glory, honor, and success. Some of us were destined to become famous world leaders, and many would find their niche in the business world with boo-coo green backs miraculously filling their pockets. What a crock of shit!

Up, up, and away went our gold-tasseled, square, blue, flattop hats with shouts of glee. Maybe the Bible is right. Miracles do happen. Fifteen of my sixteen boys had a little round tube of paper, tied with a blue and gold ribbon that informed the world we had faced the enemy, outlasted the siege, and were at last free of the fruitcake administrators.

Graduation day came and went.

Back in our hideout, the excitement gradually faded, like the eclipse of the sun. It was bright one moment, than incrementally a creeping paralysis plunged our world into darkness. Several of us had jobs through the high school co-op program. These jobs would now be made available to next year's senior class. Dave had dropped out before graduation to get a job and support the family. He was the lucky one. The rest of us didn't have a job or know what we were going to do with our lives.

We didn't like school very much, but now we were lost without it. Denby's logo was a ship's anchor that had tied us down, but we had been set free. We were floating away with nothing to stabilize our lives. We were aimlessly adrift and felt as though we were sinking into an ocean of our own making. We missed some of the teachers who had been very patient with us, who genuinely cared about us and tried to help us understand the value and need for a good education.

"What we going to do now?" asked Bruce.

No one answered.

"Anyone want a beer?" asked Bruce.

No one answered.

"How about a game of pool?" asked Bruce.

No one answered.

Bruce stomped out of the hideout and slammed the door so hard it was a wonder the glass didn't shatter into a zillion pieces.

No one said anything.

I'd heard stories about crowds of people being prodded into mass hysteria and even mass violence, but had never heard of fifteen wild-ass boys being prodded into a state of mass depression, especially after successfully winning a four-year war. We had graduated from high school and it didn't feel good.

"Let's all go home, sleep in late tomorrow, and meet here about one o'clock," I said. "Maybe tomorrow we'll feel better. We can talk about the future and make some plans."

"I don't want to be a criminal," said Ron.

"Me either," agreed George.

"I want to get married and find a job," said James.

"That's great for you guys. You've got steady girls. I don't have anyone," said Tom.

Without saying a word, Russell left. In quick order, one by one, the AFO boys left. Jake was the last to leave.

"Jake, give Bruce a call and tell him what we're doing," I said.

"Sure." And he was gone.

I sat for a long time, thinking. I smoked my pipe, a new habit I acquired that week. *I guess I'm trying to at least appear grown up. I hate this pipe. It makes my tongue burn.* I sipped on a hot stale beer. *I never did like the taste of beer. Just trying to be grown up, I guess. I should probably go into the house, but no one's home anyhow. I think I'll go for a walk.* I did. I walked until it was as dark outside as I felt inside.

The next day was a wet morning. Michigan is known for lightning and thunder storms. Waves of black clouds move in and a downpour strikes with a vengeance, flooding the streets, overwhelming the storm drains, and flowing over the curbs. Today it was different. The sky was a dribbling washboard, a chilling drizzle that soaked through the skin to saturate the innards. *Just what we need,* I thought. *A dark day to make bright plans.*

The AFO boys straggled in about two o'clock and put on a forced show of cheerfulness to impress each other and convince themselves that prospects for the future were good. They failed on both counts.

"So, boss, what's the big plan for our future?" asked Bruce.

I was surprised because I think it was the first and only time anyone called me boss. I wasn't surprised that Bruce was first to get to the point. I had hoped for a bit more time to lay the foundation for my plan, but socializing just wasn't going to be part of the day's agenda.

"Last night I went for a long walk," I said, "to think over what we could do. I agree with Ron. I don't want to be a criminal either. There's no future in stealing stuff. Sooner or later it'll get us locked up. So we don't want to do that."

"Yeah, we don't want to do that. What the hell do we want to do? That's the question." Bruce never let go of anything easily.

"Bruce, will ya just shut your damned mouth and let him talk. Who knows, you might learn something for a change," said Dave.

"You telling me to shut up?" Bruce screamed.

"Yeah, shut your big mouth," Dave shouted back.

"Enough, enough," chimed in Herman as he stepped between Bruce and Dave before their words became physical.

Bruce slipped in the last word. "What the hell are you here for anyhow? You already got a job."

Ron looked at me and calmly asked, "What ya got in mind?"

I took a deep breath and said, "Last night I saw a Navy poster that said, 'Join Together, Stay Together.' And another that said 'Uncle Sam Wants You.' I propose that we all join the Navy together and stay together. That way, we'll have something to do, make some money, see the world, and no one will mess with us."

"Not me," said James. "Marlene and I plan to get married. I don't want to be stuck on some stupid ship in the middle of the ocean."

"Me either," said Herman. "Marilyn and I are getting married too. Beside, my dad'll give me a job at the telephone company."

"I don't know," said Tom. "It might be fun. We could be dicking the girls in all the ports."

"I prefer the Army," added Dave.

With sincerity, Bruce asked, "What about your job?"

"I hate it, and I want to get out of this rat hole," said Dave.

Everyone had an opinion and no shyness in expressing it. The discussion rattled on and on for as long as I could tolerate it.

"All right, that's enough," I said. "It's my opinion that we should all join the Navy together and stay together. I'll put it to a vote just to be democratic."

"I don't care what you vote. I'm not going to join the Navy," said Herman. James joined him, but no one else refused to abide by a vote. Everyone voted to join the navy except James, Herman, and Dave.

"My dad was in the Army, and I'm joining the Army," stated Dave.

"That settles it," I announced. "Tomorrow at four o'clock, everyone be at the Navy recruiting office. It's right next to Tim's Barber Shop on Gratiot."

I didn't expect James or Herman to show, and I wasn't sure about Dave. Generally, he was fun-loving, but usually very determined once he made a decision.

There was, by AFO standards, minimal grumbling and tacit acceptance. The change in weather may have helped a little. The drizzle had stopped, and rays of sunlight forced their way through our dirty windows. Most of the guys left soon after the voting. It was one thing to bite off this momentous decision and another to chew and digest it. It would take a little time.

The next morning bounded in with sun and warmth to mend the soul. My dad promised me the use of our family car at three-thirty. Ron stopped by the clubhouse and agreed to come back later and ride with me to the recruiting office.

"Did you tell your parents what were going to do today?" I asked Ron.

"No way! They'd have locked me in my room. How about you?"

"Nope, I have two brothers who are conscientious objectors. They refused to be drafted, said they'd never kill anyone. Our government imprisoned them in concentration camps. One is in Pennsylvania working in a nut house and the other in Oregon crushing rocks to build roads. I don't think they get paid for working."

"Wow, your parents will kill you when they find out."

"No they won't. They don't believe in killing either," I said.

After Ron left, I sat a long time by myself in the hideout, thinking about my decision. I had always been so sure of my decisions, but I wasn't comfortable with this one. *Am I making a mistake? Can I kill someone if I have to? Maybe, if it's them or me. Maybe I'll never have to. Being in a submarine might be good. You don't see anyone you kill that way. Well, whatever! It's too late now, anyhow. The decision's made. It's a zipper on my body bag.*

The sun inched its way across the heavens. At three-thirty, Ron arrived and we waited on the front porch for my dad to arrive with the car. He didn't show.

"We could walk, you know," said Ron. "It'll only take us twenty minutes."

"Naw, let's wait, Dad will be here in time," I said.

At four o'clock, my dad still had not come.

"We gotta go," said Ron.

"Yeah, you better believe it. If we run we can still make it," I said.

We ran most of the way. We didn't make it. The recruiting office had closed early. No one was there. No recruiters and no boys. *This isn't going to go over very well. I should probably leave for Timbuktu.*

We bent over with hands on our knees, panting. We slid down to a sitting position and leaned against the front wall of the recruiting office.

"What are we going to do now? We're dead meat," said Ron.

Obviously the boys were going to be irate. I had talked them into joining the Navy together, and then I didn't join with them. With my index finger I pushed my glasses up the bridge of my nose. I had been forced to wear glasses from the age of five. They had stimulated the right side of my brain and my creativity. I had developed a lifestyle in which ingenuity and time made anything possible.

"What are we going to do now? Let's go to college," I said.

EPILOGUE

In 1952 we graduated from Denby High School. Several of my boys joined the Navy together, but none were kept together as promised by the recruiting posters. They were powerless and dispersed in all directions. They didn't try to do anything about it. Dave joined the Army. Herman and James got married and disappeared into oblivion. Russell committed suicide. We walked away from our high school and home turf thinking we were tough guys even though we had never badly hurt anyone.

Today I know the location of three of the sixteen plus two that are deceased. These survivors have done well, lived productive lives, raised fine families, and are enjoying pleasurable retirements, despite some of the aches and pains of old age.

The Depression, with its hard times and shortage of money, stressed families and predisposed the youth to find all kinds of ways to enhance their lives. Many were fortunate enough to climb out of the magnetic depth to a higher level of human interaction. To those who didn't make it, my heart sorrows, and to those who did, I have praise for the support rendered by others who accepted them and gave them a fighting chance. My going to college had not been planned for and there was no money to pay for it.

Lack of money was no obstacle. We enrolled anyhow. Ron and I went to college together, admitted on probationary status. We immediately found employment and began earning our way. Ron left after the first year and joined the Air Force. He served our country as a bombardier and honorably retired with the rank of Lieutenant Colonel.

My college life was as checkered as earlier elementary and high school life had been. I had completed the eighth grade without learning to read or write. It had taken a parent-principal conference to pave my way into Denby High School, where I was expelled for getting into trouble by raising the grand curtain. In a repeat performance, I was expelled from college twice for failing English 101 three times.

During my first year in college I adopted a lifestyle quote. I think it came from Huckleberry Finn, but I don't know for sure who said it or the exact words. It goes like this: The race does not always go to the swift, but to those who keep running. I was determined to keep running and outlast the shortsightedness of the Fruitcake who told me I would never be able to graduate from college. I did graduate. It took me five years to do four years of work and acquire a bachelor's degree with a major in Social Science, a minor in Psychology. It took another five years to complete a four year program and earn a master's degree in Theology with an exegetical major featuring Hebrew and Greek. I believe this is not too shabby for someone who to this very day cannot spell and doesn't know English punctuation or grammar. I slowly climbed my way out of my childhood and teenage ways into the sunlight for a better viewpoint of the world and humanity.

It is no surprise that techniques learned during youthful gang days were effectively employed during my college tenure. After ten years of college, a part-time working wife, and two children under the age of six, I was able to graduate without one cent of college debt. It was easy to do.

The city of Columbus, Ohio advertised for a Senior Electrical Engineer. I had no knowledge of electricity or an engineering education, but I took the test anyhow. I failed it better than most others failed. I memorized the questions. My engineering student frat house roommate gave me the answers. I retook the test and was hired as a senior electrical draftsman, one grade lower than the engineering designation they sought. My roommate daily instructed me in what to do at work the next day to fulfill the job responsibilities. I made good money.

North American Aviation had an opening for an engineer. I applied. They could not resist hiring a Columbus City-employed electrical draftsman. Under their banner, I designed the temperature and pressurization system for the pilot and navigator cockpit of the A3J, Vigilante, a Mach-three Navy attack bomber. I was rewarded with a super salary.

Bonny Floyd steel mill had a position available for running the BataTron, which used uranium and cobalt to x-ray casting for atomic reactors. I was told there were only two BataTrons in the world and only a dozen people who were qualified to operate them. I offered to work the job for free for three days with the understanding that if I could proficiently operate the equipment that they would give me the job. They bit, I learned, they hired, and again I had a super income.

During my college days, I adopted two additional guiding principles that became my compass for traveling through adult life. One was advocated by my frat house roommate, who became tired of my childish prankster behavior and mouthing off inappropriately. He gave me three words and told me each was the Hebrew name representing the specialty for one of the tribes of Israel. They were: Mishma, Dumah, and Massa.

Mishma was supposed to be the tribe of counselors, i.e. the listeners; Dumah were the intellectuals, the thinkers; and the Massa tribe were the peacemakers. I was advised to consider these tribes when I was tempted to inappropriately say what I was thinking.

In my roommate's words, "I want you to shut up and listen. Listen intently. Then, shut up and think about it, think deeply about what you've heard, and finally, if you feel it's necessary to say something, then say it in such a way as to create peace and not animosity."

It was good advice. I engraved these three words on a plastic plaque and have carried it in my pocket for the past fifty years. Many times I've put my hand into my pocket, run my fingers across the letters, and reminded myself of these guiding principles. I began to grow out of my gang behavior mindset.

The other life-guiding principle came from my nemesis: an English class. It is a quote from Waldo Emerson, which I paraphrase for simplicity.

Emerson said: "Say today what you think today, and say tomorrow what you think tomorrow, even if what you say tomorrow contradicts what you say today." Isn't that neat? For me it meant: Think intently, be willing to speak, keep thinking, be willing to be wrong, correct previous pronouncements, and thereby be true to your own conscience and honest with others.

I will always be thankful for my parents who instilled in me a wholesome faith in God and my discovery of the three guiding principles which provided a foundation for my growth. First: The winner is not always the fastest, but the one who keeps running. Secondly: Listen intently, think deeply, speak with the intent of peace, and third: Accept and acknowledge the fact that you can be wrong, and thus be true to your own conscience and everyone you deal with.

America is a country where everyone has a chance to be better than their environment indicates is possible. For me it started with spiritual and loving parents, an adjunct of close brotherhood in family and friends, a string of dedicated teachers, and a gradual realization through hands-on experiences that life could be better if I detected and accepted the opportunities that came my way. My growth was incrementally slow, but steady.

I recently learned that history had recreated itself. In 1954, while Ron and I were in college, Ron's sister Robin was walking in my footsteps, at least as far as organizing her cohorts into a club of like-minded youth. Prior to graduating from Robinson Elementary School, she organized ten of her girl friends into what she referred to as a Sorority. They called themselves OFA Decem. The OFA was for AFO backward and the Decem was Greek for ten. Their Sorority name was condensed to the OFA D's when they entered Denby High School. Since graduation from Denby in 1958, they have regularly held OFA D reunions.

FAMILY HISTORY

My dad, Elmer Clarence Labuhn, was born in Detroit, Michigan. He is a descendant of the French/German Huguenots, a term used to describe a growing contingent of Calvinist Protestants, many of whom cloistered for self-preservation in the border towns of La Rochelle and Samcerre, France from 1572 to 1578 during the Bartholomew Massacre. The Catholics were intent on a massive slaughter of these rebel Protestants.

Many of the survivors escaped into Germany. Grandpa Edward Labuhn's birth place on his daughters Evelyn's birth certificate is Lauenburg, a farming community, now named LeBork. It was part of Pomerania in Prussia. and is now in Poland. Grandma Olga Zimmerman's birth place is listed on her daughter Evelyn's birth certificate as Merienwerden, Prussia in Pomerania and is now called Kwidzyn in Poland.

The town of Labun, located in Pomerania, was also known as Labuhn for a brief time. The "h" signifies the family-owned property. The relationship between these towns and my family history is only speculation, as we have no firm documentation to support a direct connection. Today, Labun is located in Poland and is renamed Labounia. In 1880, my dad's grandparents, along with their brood of children, migrated to the United States from Pomerania.

In 1920, Elmer married Clara Hay, a tea-sipping lady of Scot/Canadian descent, born in Minto, North Dakota. They moved into a home in the country just outside the fast-growing shipping and industrial town of Detroit. The country setting soon became a thriving community, and the street on which my parents lived was renamed from Rochdale to Rochelle. They lived there until they died.

I had three older brothers: Richard, Floyd, and Gerald. The oldest, Richard, was artistically oriented, loving photography, theater, and, uncharacteristically, his Harley Davidson motorcycle. The second oldest, Floyd, was an electronics expert and an artist painting with oils. Gerald was theologically predisposed and spent his life in the Lutheran Ministry caring for the needs of orphans, elderly nursing home residents, and raising a brood of six beautiful children. My brothers all settled down in one geographical location for their life endeavors. Unlike my brothers, I am the wondering gypsy intent on experiencing life in as many states as possible. At 79 years of age, I'm still called the baby of the family. I guess I've never really grown up.

My brother Floyd told me that Dad was a wrestler prior to being married. I cannot guarantee that this is true. However, I can certify that on one occasion Floyd sassed Dad at the dinner table, Dad stood up, and Floyd became a jet stream escaping through the closed screened front door. Dad calmly sat down and continued to eat his mashed potatoes, after mixing them with two spoons full of peas.

My mom was a quiet woman who never raised her voice or scolded her brood of four active boys. Her social life centered on line tap dancing with the girls at Robinson Elementary School. We were a tea totaling family, never having more than sherry for cooking in the house. When I was about seven years of age, I caught Mom taking a sip of sherry. She was embarrassed and made me promise not to tell dad. She was deeply in love with Dad and often sat on his lap with her arms around his neck.

My dad's older sister, my Aunt Edna, was a major intellectual influence in my life. She was head of the Speech Correction Department of the Detroit Public School system, a founding member of the League of Women Voters, spoke several languages, served as tutor for immigrants coming into our country, was a lover of classical music and opera, and drove me nuts constantly correcting my grammar. She took me to see "Porgy and Bess" and became angry at me for trying to make out with a little girl in the next seat rather than paying attention to the drama on stage.

Aunt Edna's husband, Ted Geeson, supervised Detroit housing developments for the poor. One development was decimated by tornadoes that roared through the area, leveling over half the housing and removing the roof the Greyhound bus storage and repair terminal. I considered Edna and Ted to be my wealthy relatives, whose only youthful charge was a big fat cat. They were our Santa Claus, annually delivering wonderful gifts every Christmas.

Economically, we were not poor folks. Dad worked for the United States Postal Service, so we had a steady income through the 1930 Great Depression years. We had enough money to fill our coal bin through a basement window. We fired up the furnace twice a day, once in the early morning and once late at night. When the fire went out, it got cold, really cold. Snow blew in around the edges of my attic bedroom window, but my blankets were deeper than the snow.

Prior to the death of my parents, the City of Detroit passed an ordinance that no home could be sold without first having all the wiring and plumbing changed to copper. It would cost us more to fix the house than it would sell for. It took us four years to give it away. In 1986, after my parents passed away, my inheritance was less than $400.00, but my family life has been rich.

PUFFED UP DEFINITIONS

CHRONICLE: A year ago I was chatting over a mug of beer with Mike McNeff, a celebrated mystery writer and former police officer and attorney. I mentioned that in my youth I had been a gang leader. He asked, "Why did you ever organize a gang?" He nearly fell off the bar stool laughing when he heard my answer. "You have a story to tell," he said. So I did, a story about my gang, with adjustments to compensate for my faulty memory, and spiced with minimal creativity. These episodes had been my guarded secret for over sixty-five years.

GANGS: It's important that you have an accurate perception of what a gang consists of. Today the word "gang" conjures up images of nasty, depraved, violent, corrupt, gun-toting, fist-punching, drug-dealing, sex-orientated, no-good bastard criminals.

The gangs I was familiar with, in the 1940s, did not fit this description. The Harper Gang and the Seven Mile Road Gang may have exhibited some of these characteristics on rare occasions. It was rumored that they threw an enemy through a storefront window and stuffed someone upside down in a garbage can just for fun.

The gang activities in my repertoire couldn't compete with the nasty standards of today, nor did they have access to the array of knowledge or deadly weaponry presently available. A pipe wrench in the hands of a 1940s gang member was viewed the same as a gun is viewed in the hands of a thug today.

Gangs come in all shapes, sizes and colors; their behavior patterns vary from a group of fun-loving, good fellows to the extreme of depraved psychopaths. Scholarly Webster tells us a gang is a group of people associated together in some way. For youth, Webster states, gangs are from one neighborhood banded together for social reasons and often are a band of juvenile delinquents.

We didn't consider ourselves a gang, but it is true that we were independent, not affiliated with any officially recognized federal, state, or community organization.

GANG LEADERS: Gang leader styles come in every form imaginable, ranging from the use of fear and physical force to passive manipulation. Gang leader recognition also comes in many forms, ranging from the highly visible ego maniac to the camouflaged mastermind that makes recognition of the leader difficult. This memoir illustrated only one gang and one leadership style: my gang and my style.

As for my leadership style, I was so passive that, at times, I wondered if I was truly a gang leader and whether the boys recognize me as such. I had assembled the initial members, written the formal structure documents, provided a physical facility to hangout, and on the cover page of our photo album I had specified rules for borrowing. The page was signed "Your President, G.M. Labuhn." My style had a flare for formality.

FRUITCAKES: This term referring to school administrators, implies a negative attitude toward these individuals. We actually held them in high regard because of their position of authority, but we did see them as figures vulnerable for harassment. We viewed school administrators differently than the teachers. We had teachers we appreciated: one of the boys was even in love with a math teacher, and two guys were interested in becoming teachers.

There were so many gangs causing turmoil in Detroit in the 1940s that the Fruitcakes in the school system outlawed their existence. The school's edict did little more than drive gangs underground.

FRENCH WORDS: There are a few French words in this memoir that are intentionally misspelled to provide consistency with the nature of the setting and of the gang culture. These French expressions are written as they sounded, since we had never seen them in print.

FUZZ BALLS: The terms Fuzz Balls, referring to the police, also implies a negative attitude toward these individuals. We actually held them in high regard, but we did see them as authority figures vulnerable for harassment. Several of my boys were interested in becoming police officers.

GENEOLOGY: This is a story of one phase of one life, at one point in history connected to one family's genealogical skeleton. As an adjunct to depicting youthful life in Detroit in the 1940s, recording these episodes hangs tidbits of personal information on the bones of the past, adding a human touch to sterile names on a chart to enhance my family's historical lineage.

There is some relatively "bad" language in this book. To my knowledge, I am the only member of my family that used words that at the time were consider foul language. Other members of my family may have said some unsavory things at times of stress, anger, or pain, but I never heard them and they never heard me.

This memoir reveals my secret life on the fringe of the family circle. My life within the family, while not detailed in this memoir, was filled with love, patience, and understanding. We didn't money reserves, fancy clothes, or all of the dysfunctional problems that plague so many families today. My brothers, Richard and Floyd, now deceased, and Gerald, who is competing with me to see who can live the longest, are the finest brothers anyone could ever have. My family was a treasure cup that will never drain dry.

SERIOUSNESS: I thought my boys and our activities were serious business. In reflection, what I thought was tough was little more than child's play in comparison to today's perceptions. I wonder how or why we survived some of our misadventures. Perhaps it's testimony to the good fortune that walks hand in hand with youthful stupidity.

SWITCH BLADE: A Switch Blade was the meanest weapon of choice for many gangs in the 1940s. It was considered quick, effective, and silent. It is similar to a pocket knife in that it has a blade which folds into the knife handle. It is different is several critical ways. The blade is spring loaded, and flashes open in a tenth of a second following a push of the opening button. It locks in the open position and cannot be closed without twisting a blade closing lever. The blade is sharp pointed at the end. There is a locking safety mechanism to prevent it from accidently opening when in a pocket. I am told they are different if you're right or left handed, but I've never seen one for a lefty. The typical switch blade, when open, is nine inches long.

Effectively using a switch blade takes a little practice, and carelessness can badly wound the user, rather than the intended enemy. The typical use of a switch blade is to mortally stab another individual. It requires practicing a pendulum swinging of the arm, holding the blade with no fingers protruding over the edge of the closed blade, and synchronized timing so as not to stab oneself in the leg when the blade swings past the leg in route to the stomach of the intended victim.

TRUTH: The episodes in *My Gang* are true, though the names have been changed to protect the guilty. I assure you that I don't have Alzheimer's, even though I have stashed 79 years of joyous living under my belt. I confess that I don't remember who said what or the exact words they used. As an author, I have taken the liberty to be creative when necessary in order to convey the drama experienced. Additionally, I am not aware of all the things the members of our band of merry boys did, and some of them may not remember the episodes that bubble to the surface for me.

This memoir depicts the mood of the time as accurately as I can recall. It is a snapshot of my youth as lived seven miles northeast of the center of Detroit.

Unfortunately, or perhaps fortunately, depending on your mind set, the episodes in the life of one group of youth in Detroit would be told differently if they had been written at the time the events occurred. It was both fun and frustrating to write this story seventy years after the events. The mood of the book is comical and often dangerous, but it was serious living at the time.

ANOTHER BOOK
BY GORDON M. LABUHN

Murder Has Two Faces A killer is hiding behind a false face, murdering ill prison inmates so that guilty prisoners on death row can walk to freedom and complete their threats to kill the judge. The reader is challenged to detect the clues and figure out who the killer is before being revealed in the story. One prisoner beats the system and is released.

Special Appreciation to the following celebrated authors for critiquing this memoir during its development. Their unrelenting encouragement made it possible for me to gain insights into hidden aspects of my teenage life, as well as giving me courage to make known events that were shrouded by shame and never made known to anyone. The absurdity of the serious was transformed into a reality of humor. The historical mores of city life are depicted as experienced.

Mike McNeff, Author of ***GOTU***: A police, crime action adventure involving a special narcotics squad, dangerous drug couriers, a prominent drug overlord, and a revenge kidnapping of the daughter of the squad's leader. In the fight to rescue the daughter, there are no rules.

Dorothy Read, Author of ***End the Silence*:** living history through the eyes of Ilse Evelijn Veere Smit, whose childhood is shattered when the Japanese take over the Dutch East Indies in 1942. The story takes her through the horror of a Japanese concentration camp on her home island of Java, the terror of the Indonesian revolution that follows, and the trauma of living in a family that refuses to talk about it.

M. G. Chapman, Author of **Covert Ops: License2Chill:** An ex SEAL explosive expert and a cocky womanizing ex-Navy fighter pilot are a deeply embedded covert ops team assigned to eliminate an extortionist who is threatening to destroy most of the planet's population. A beautiful psychological profiler provides insight and guidance in tracking down the evil mastermind. The team discovers the weapon of mass destruction isn't what they expected…it's worse, much worse. Chapman is an ex-naval air officer with an MBA in marketing.

ABOUT THE AUTHOR

Gordon's education through high school was hampered by poor eyesight, resulting in deficits in spelling, grammar, and punctuation. In the 1940s he and sixteen comrades, known as Club AFO, roamed the streets that bordered the inner city of Detroit. He struggled through college, and after being expelled for failing English 101 twice, he obtained a BA degree, majoring in Social Science from Capital University, and a Master of Divinity Degree from the Lutheran Theological Seminary in Columbus, Ohio.

He served as Executive Director of non-profit organizations for 21 years and Chief Executive Officer for proprietary for-profit corporation for five years. He also spent three years in government services.

As a writer and producer, his works include twelve one-hour religious vignettes and a nationally publicized movie that featured an all-teenage cast. Gordon authored "Planning Effective Meetings," published by Northern Michigan University in the 1960s. He was a feature article writer for a Detroit-area newspaper, winner of the National PR/PI award for the youth Health Behavior Inventory project, winner of the Whidbey Island Bayview Classic Auto writing competition, is published in "The Dog with The Old Soul," and authored "Murder Has Two Faces" in 2011.

Gordon is an active member of the Whidbey Island Writers Association, The Mystery Writers of American, Andrea Hurst's "Just Write" consortium, and the Whidbey Writers Group. He and his wife, Karen, reside on Whidbey Island, Washington, and have three children David, Kevin, Ashley, and one deceased son, Gregory.

19663502R00101

Made in the USA
Charleston, SC
05 June 2013